Perfect
Peace

SELWYN HUGHES

Perfect Peace

POCKET DEVOTIONS

January/February
The Nature of the Spiritual Journey

March/April
Complete in Christ

May/June
The Burning, Cleansing Flame

July/August
Wisdom for Living

September/October
His Story – Our Story

November/December
Revealed by Name

Divine discipleship

FOR READING AND MEDITATION
2 CORINTHIANS 3:1–18

*'And we, who ... all reflect the Lord's glory, are being
transformed into his likeness with ever-increasing glory ...'*
(v.18)

Though we do not all travel along the road of
discipleship at the same rate, I believe there is a
divine pattern at work. While the Holy Spirit respects
our individuality since every person is different, there are
certain stages and experiences through which we must
all go for spiritual formation to take place. The phrase
'spiritual formation' simply means God's creation of
the image of Christ within us. God is so excited about
Jesus that He wants to make everyone like Him. It is the
way God goes about the task of producing the image of
Christ in us, and the stages we have to go through –
stages which are common to us all – that we shall seek
to discover as we start another year.

*Father God, on this first day of a new year I ask that You
will help me to journey with You so I become more like Your
Son. Amen.*

'Are you saved?'

FOR READING AND MEDITATION
LUKE 24:1–35

'Were not our hearts burning within us while he talked with us on the road and opened the Scriptures to us?' (v.32)

One of the things some Christians fail to understand is that when we become followers of Jesus Christ we are just starting out on a spiritual journey. We are saved when, by faith, we receive the salvation God offers to those who believe that Jesus was sacrificed to take the punishment due to us. But saying we are saved may make it sound as if all the work has been done. Although we are saved from the penalty of sin we are not totally saved from the power of sin (because we do still sin) and we are definitely not saved from the presence of sin. The Christian life is more than making a one-off commitment. We are on a transformational journey that will lead us to a deeper understanding of the Lord.

Lord Jesus, as we journey together, open up the Scriptures to me, reveal Your glory and make Yourself known to me. Amen.

'A gospel of sin management'

FOR READING AND MEDITATION
ROMANS 12:1–21

'Do not conform any longer to the pattern of this world, but be transformed by the renewing of your mind.' (v.2)

In his book, *The Divine Conspiracy*, Dallas Willard comments that for many Christians, 'The current gospel becomes a gospel of sin management'. In other words, Christians become preoccupied with the problem of sin that keeps occurring in their lives. This is an important issue but there is much more to the Christian life. As Christians we have embarked on a transformational journey during which we should be passing from one degree of glory to another. As Paul puts it in 2 Corinthians 3:18: 'But all of us who are Christians have no veils on our faces, but reflect like mirrors the glory of the Lord. We are transfigured, and the transformation comes from the Lord who is the Spirit in ever-increasing splendour into his own image' (J.B. Phillips).

Father, thank You that You love me so much, and that by Your Spirit You seek to transform me into the image of Your own dear Son. Amen.

The long walk

FOR READING AND MEDITATION
JOHN 1:1–18

*'From the fulness of his grace we have all received one
blessing after another.' (v.16)*

Thinking back to my youth, I recall how we would talk
repeatedly about our conversion experience and try
to recapture the emotion. Walking to the front of the
church as a sign of your decision to follow Jesus can be
a wonderful thing. Not so long ago I went back to the
church where I was converted and stood on the spot
where I found Christ. When the Spirit of God gripped
me and I walked to the front of the church what I didn't
know, and no one told me, was that the walk didn't end
there but would continue through the whole of my life.
Have we been too focused on exuberant beginnings and
victorious endings, forgetting the slow unravelling of
God's grace that takes place along our journey?

*O God, may I not forget the moment when You so
wonderfully stepped into my life, but may I not forget either
that You're not finished with me yet! Amen.*

'Microwave Christianity'

FOR READING AND MEDITATION
LUKE 15:11–32

'So he got up and went to his father.' (v.20)

One writer says that there are three phases through which God takes us: the purgative phase (cleansing of sin), the illuminative phase (the revelation of God's Word), and the unitive phase (a closer communion with God). The realisation that I was on a journey – a transformational journey – revolutionised my whole way of thinking. Our life is one of 'becoming', not simply 'doing'. It is a process of transformation. The trouble with many Christians these days is that they are in too much of a hurry when it comes to spiritual formation. Someone has called them 'microwave Christians'. They want everything to happen in a few minutes rather than being willing to take the slow, sure approach to transformation.

O God, help me this day to be totally focused on You and not distracted by the things of the world. Amen.

The journey of life

FOR READING AND MEDITATION
DEUTERONOMY 10:12–22

'... *what does the* Lord *your God ask of you but to fear the* Lord *your God ...*' (v.12)

Almost all the great saints of the past recognised that life is a journey, and that on the journey there are steps which every Christian must take. I have identified eight of these steps. That isn't to say there aren't more, but certainly not less. The first of these is acceptance of the fact that we need to develop biblical holiness. While considering this subject, my mind went back to a very godly man who, during the early years of my Christian life, sat me down and said, 'Selwyn, do you realise God's primary goal for you is not to make you happy but to make you holy? It's not a matter of happiness first and holiness if possible. Holiness must come first and happiness will then be a consequence.'

O Father, I see that holiness is something I cannot have too much of – I cannot be too much like You or have too much of Your holiness. Amen.

Ambassadors for Christ

FOR READING AND MEDITATION
ISAIAH 6:1–13

'With it he touched my mouth and said, "See, this has touched your lips; your guilt is taken away and your sin atoned for."' (v.7)

Holiness is, I believe, the first thing the Holy Spirit wants to impart to us as we set out on our personal spiritual journey, which brings us closer to God. *Because God is holy we must be holy too.* The deep desire to be rid of sin, and the eagerness to pursue holiness, is characteristic of all who long for a close relationship with God. It is evident that we are walking in holiness when we are no longer comfortable with sin. Sin becomes less attractive as we grow more attracted to God's ways, which are far higher than ours. Holiness is a sign that we have been set apart by God for His purpose. If we are to be Christ's ambassadors then our lives must be holy, otherwise we are misrepresenting Him.

Lord God, help me and teach me how to make holiness a way of life and truly represent Christ as His ambassador. Amen.

Growing by gazing

FOR READING AND MEDITATION
PSALM 99:1–9

'Exalt the LORD our God and worship at his footstool; he is holy.' (v.5)

In the soul of every Christian there is something that responds to what is holy. Experience has shown me that the best way to understand holiness is to gaze steadily at Jesus Christ and consult one's heart and mind at the reaction one feels. Never did a human form hold One so pure, so adorable, so holy. This adoring contemplation of the Saviour has been called 'the secret of the saints'. Their biographies show them to be people who did not just devote themselves to constant probing or asking endless questions of the Bible. Instead they looked in love and longing at Jesus. And their holiness was a by-product of this contemplation. They grew in holiness as they grew in the steadiness and fixity of their gazing.

Father, may I receive a vision of the moral majesty and purity of the One who is divine. Deepen my understanding of all this. Amen.

Boiled alive

FOR READING AND MEDITATION
EXODUS 3:1–22

'"Do not come any closer," God said. "Take off your sandals, for the place where you are standing is holy ground."' (v.5)

Statistics show there has been a sharp decline in church attendance. One explanation is this: the Church has lost its prophetic edge due to a lack of teaching on the nature of God's holiness and the implications this has for our lives. Yes, God is love, but He is *holy* love. The UK Church is going through a phase that is best called 'gradualism'. Let me illustrate by telling you about a frog. When the frog was put into boiling water it understandably jumped out. But when it was put in cold water, and the heat was increased gradually, it adapted to the temperature until it was boiled alive! We are in danger of being brainwashed by the world – not only by its post-Christian ideas but also by its lifestyle.

O Father, if ever Your Church needed a fresh vision of Your holiness it is today. Fill our pulpits with prophets and teachers who have a knowledge of the holy, loving God. In Christ's name. Amen.

Almost innocent

FOR READING AND MEDITATION
JOSHUA 24:14–28

'… then choose for yourselves this day whom you will serve …' (v.15)

I n his book *The Great Divorce* C.S. Lewis describes a young man who is tormented by a red lizard that sits on his shoulder and mocks him. The man hates the lizard yet hesitates to have it killed. For Lewis, this typifies the tendency we all have to compromise and allow indwelling sin in our lives. 'It's almost innocent,' we say to ourselves as we try to justify holding on to the things we know are wrong but are reluctant to part with. And with such words we allow the lizards that torment us to live. Yet what seems almost innocent is, in fact, deadly. We are living in a day when holiness is a word that is missing in the Church's vocabulary. The situation is serious.

O God, may Your holiness reveal the insidious disease of sin that is deep within me. Help me surrender to Your great love today. Amen.

Hardened hearts

FOR READING AND MEDITATION
EPHESIANS 4:1–19

*'They are ... separated from the life of God because of ...
the hardening of their hearts.' (v.18)*

We are living in an age in which sin, as C.S. Lewis said, is regarded as 'almost innocent'. The Gentiles were living in the futility of their thinking (v.17); they thought there was fulfilment in the way they were going, but there was not. What appeared 'almost innocent' would prove to be deadly. This darkened understanding was caused by their stubbornness and resistance to the things of God. They were given opportunities to change, but they would not change. The choices they made may have seemed almost innocent, but they resulted in hearts that were hardened. And hardened hearts alienate us from the life of God and bring about spiritual death.

Father, keep my heart soft and my eyes always turned towards You so that the 'almost innocent' things will not enter my life and separate me from You. Amen.

Epidemic numbness

FOR READING AND MEDITATION
EPHESIANS 4:17–32

'... they have given themselves over to sensuality so as to indulge in every kind of impurity, with a continual lust for more.' (v.19)

Paul warns us what will happen to those with hardened hearts. In our society today there are issues that are almost epidemic amongst us. Thousands are hooked on pornography, gambling and other addictions. We are living in an age when the inducements to sin are many, and they crowd in on us from all directions. The deadened soul requires a greater level of stimulation to arouse it. This is the downward spiral of any addiction. Can this be proved? Consider television dramas over the years. Programmes that were considered shocking to an earlier audience are now regarded as relatively harmless. What can seem almost innocent is, in reality, creating an addiction for greater and greater forms of depravity.

O God, help me to hide Your Word in my heart so that I might not sin against You. Guard my spirit, soul and body. Amen.

Riding with horses

FOR READING AND MEDITATION
DEUTERONOMY 30:1–20

'… I call heaven and earth as witnesses … I have set before you life and death, blessings and curses. Now choose life …' (v.19)

Returning to C.S. Lewis's story of the red lizard, the man finally agrees to allow an angel to help, and the angel throws it to the ground, dead. But when it hits the ground, an amazing thing happens; it turns into a stallion, and the young man rides away with great joy. What has been the ruler now becomes the ruled. What has ridden him, he now rides. What does it mean to ride with horses? We need to make the right decisions and we need to examine our lives for the presence of sin. If we are not asking 'Lord, what are the things in my life that are hardening my heart and so denying my mind the light of Your life?' then we are allowing ourselves to become terribly vulnerable to sin's deadly effects.

Heavenly Father, give me the courage and strength to choose You this day. Amen.

Don't drink the water

FOR READING AND MEDITATION
MATTHEW 13:1–23

'For this people's heart has become calloused; they hardly hear with their ears, and they have closed their eyes.' (v.15)

I once read about the sinking of the battle cruiser *USS Indianapolis* at the end of World War II. A Japanese torpedo hit the cruiser and it sank within minutes; 300 of the 1,200 men died; 900 went into the sea. After four days and five nights without fresh water only 316 of these men survived. Those who perished died because they drank the seawater despite medical officers remonstrating with them and telling them not to do so. The apostle Paul warns us of the danger of this world's waters in Ephesians 4:17–19. In effect he is saying, 'Don't drink the waters of this world. They might look inviting, and for a moment they will seem to slake your thirst, but in the end they will destroy you.'

Thank You, Lord Jesus, that You have given us the promise that streams of living water will flow from within anyone who believes in You. Amen.

No power failure

FOR READING AND MEDITATION
EPHESIANS 1:1–23

'I pray ... that you may know ... his incomparably great power for us who believe.' (vv.18–19)

Another stage on our spiritual journey and the second aspect of our movement towards God is developing an understanding of suffering. The difficulty of reconciling the issue of suffering with the teaching that God is love is said to have produced more atheists and agnostics than any other matter. Rabbi Kushner argues that sin has so disrupted God's universe that although God is still love, His power has been diminished and He is unable to do what He longs to do. Theologically, the rabbi is a million miles off the right track. God never experiences a power failure. Today's text is just one of countless verses in the Bible which show that God's power has not in any way been diminished by sin's presence.

Father, I realise that I am looking into the heart of one of the deepest mysteries of the universe – suffering and pain. Help me in Jesus' name. Amen.

Jesus – our Overcomer

FOR READING AND MEDITATION
REVELATION 19:1–10

'Hallelujah! Salvation and glory and power belong to our God …' (v.1)

When Dr W.E. Sangster was a boy, he went to a camp. While there his father did not respond to his telegrams for more money. His friends teased him, 'Your father doesn't love you.' Later Sangster said the answer he gave then was the answer he gave to everyone who asked him for light on the subject of suffering: 'I know I'm loved and I don't know why He didn't reply. I'll wait until I get home and He will tell me Himself.' Although we cannot explain fully why a loving God allows suffering, we know without any doubt that suffering plays a vital part in the development of the soul. Jesus warned us that we would suffer for our testimony to Him. 'In this world you will have trouble' He said (John 16:33). But remember, Jesus has overcome the world.

Lord God, may I never forget that Jesus has overcome the world. Whatever problems lie ahead, they are not as great as the power behind me. Amen.

The inevitability of suffering

FOR READING AND MEDITATION
JOB 5:1–18

'Yet man is born to trouble as surely as sparks fly upward.' (v.7)

M any believe God should spare those who are good-living from troubles. The Fall has spoilt this world, and though much about it is still beautiful, accidents, calamities and suffering prevail. And these will continue until the time when God brings all things to a conclusion. Though prayer does move God to work supernaturally in some situations, life will go on being more 'tragic than orderly' until Christ returns. When Jesus hung upon the cross, the crowd cried, 'He trusted in God; let Him deliver Him' (Matt. 27:43, NKJV). God did not deliver Him; *He did something better*. And it is along this line of 'something better' that we must search in order to find the Christian solution to the problem of suffering.

Lord Jesus, I am so thankful for the cross. What is my suffering compared to that? Blessed be Your name for ever. Amen.

Monumental moments

FOR READING AND MEDITATION
PSALM 119:49–56

'My comfort in my suffering is this: Your promise preserves my life.' (v.50)

In *A Twentieth Century Testimony* the writer and broadcaster Malcolm Muggeridge records how, surprisingly, he gained particular satisfaction from looking back on experiences which, when they occurred, seemed painful and distressing. Perhaps even more surprising is the fact that he claims that everything he had learned in life which had been of benefit had been through anguish and not through happiness. 'If it were ever possible to eliminate the cold hard winds of life,' he writes, 'the result would not make life delectable but make it too banal and too trivial to be endurable. Every happening … is a parable whereby God speaks to us, and the art of life is to get the message.'

Father, set me free today from the tyranny of trying to fathom the unfathomable. No longer will I struggle to understand – I shall just stand. Amen.

A wounded healer

FOR READING AND MEDITATION
HEBREWS 2:1–18

'… it was fitting that God … should make the author of their salvation perfect through suffering.' (v.10)

As a result of all the emotional and physical suffering I have experienced, I have gained a deeper compassion for those in need and an increasing awareness that just as Christ was made perfect through suffering – in other words, brought to the glory that God intended – so I too, through suffering and submission to God, am being brought closer to perfection and the fulfilment of God's plans for my life. What has that done to me? It has transformed my life, deepened my message, given me a sensitivity to others and a new note in my ministry. I am a wounded healer. From experience I can say that though I have hated the pain, the rewards of suffering are of infinite value.

Lord Jesus, You turned Your pain to good account; help me to strengthen myself in You to do the same. Amen.

Different perspective

FOR READING AND MEDITATION
JOB 1:13–22

'At this, Job got up and tore his robe and shaved his head.
Then he fell to the ground in worship …' (v.20)

I have experienced miraculous healing myself when given just a few days to live and I have seen many wonderful miracles through my ministry. But the years have given me a different perspective. God can and does heal but not everyone experiences healing and I have often asked myself: what should be my attitude to suffering? After much thought on the matter I have become convinced that it should be one of worship. I am always challenged when I read the opening chapter of the book of Job. After receiving the tragic news of the death of his servants, sons and daughters, and the loss of all his possessions, today's text tells us that Job fell on his knees and worshipped.

O Father, may I, like Job, accept all suffering with grace and not a grudge. In Jesus' name I ask this. Amen.

Bitter or better

FOR READING AND MEDITATION
1 PETER 4:1–19

'Therefore, since Christ suffered in his body, arm yourselves also with the same attitude …' (v.1)

I have to admit that despite fully accepting the idea that there is meaning behind suffering, I still have some way to go in the matter of responding correctly to it. John Stott says, 'I sometimes wonder if the real test of our hunger for holiness is our willingness to experience any degree of suffering if only thereby God will make us holy.' I wonder too! Being a Christian does not exempt us from suffering. Have you ever noticed how the same thing can happen to two different people yet have an entirely different effect upon them? Sorrow and suffering will make some bitter while it makes others better. A similar situation but with opposite effects. The difference is our attitude.

O God, may I never forget that You are my refuge and strength, an ever-present help in trouble, and live in the light of that truth today. Amen.

Soul-making

FOR READING AND MEDITATION
PSALM 103:8–18

'For as high as the heavens are above the earth, so great is his love for those who fear him …' (v.11)

Does God heal and free us from our physical suffering? Yes He does, but sometimes He does not, for reasons known only to Himself. Even the wisest human mind is so limited in His sight. I was once healed when I had just days to live. But in more recent years I have also suffered sufficiently severely to even make me doubt God's previous intervention. When nobody suffers, nobody cares. Lighthouses are built out of drowned sailors; maimed motorists widen roads. C.S. Lewis used the wonderful term 'soul-making' in connection with this observation: 'I have seen men for the most part grow better, not worse, with advancing years.' Suffering is not good in itself, but can contribute to our good when used by God.

Heavenly Father, I can allow the disappointments of life to either move me towards You or away from You. Help me draw closer. Amen.

God is good

FOR READING AND MEDITATION
2 CORINTHIANS 11:16–32

'Five times I received from the Jews the forty lashes minus one. Three times I was beaten with rods, once I was stoned ...' (vv.24–25)

The cross does not solve the problem of suffering, but it helps us to put it into the right perspective. We may say that suffering is unjust. But life is not just for we live in a sin-stained world. At the heart of the Christian faith there is a cross, and that is the world's supreme injustice. Paul highlights some of the injustices he experienced. However, he allowed those hardships to make him more dependent on God. 'All things work together for good to those who love God,' he said (Rom. 8:28, NKJV). The happening itself may not be good, but God works in it to bring about our eternal good. That is the power of the cross. In the Lord's presence, I have learned that even in suffering God is good.

Lord Jesus, bring me to that wonderful place at the foot of Your cross where I see Your suffering turn injustice into something of spiritual benefit. Amen.

Blessings or blisters?

FOR READING AND MEDITATION
PSALM 41:1–13

'Even my close friend, whom I trusted, he who shared my bread, has lifted up his heel against me.' (v.9)

We have considered holiness and the issue of suffering. Now we move on to the issue of interpersonal relationships. The spiritual journey is not one that we are meant to walk alone. God intends us to travel in the company of other people. For some this is a wonderful arrangement; for others it is not so wonderful. People can be helpful or they can be hurtful; they can bless us or they can blister us. Ernest Hemingway said, 'We have to distrust each other; it is our only defence against betrayal.' God does not call us to live in distrust, but to live by faith in Jesus Christ. We are disciples of the One who knows what it is to be betrayed. And through His grace we can be victors, and not victims.

Father, may I grasp this truth that I cannot act in isolation, for I am bound up with my redeemed brothers and sisters. Amen.

We are not alone

FOR READING AND MEDITATION
GENESIS 45:1–25

'Then he threw his arms around his brother Benjamin and wept, and Benjamin embraced him, weeping.' (v.14)

I initially thought that the Christian walk was with Jesus alone. So I had a great surprise when I discovered that by receiving Jesus into my life I inherited His family also, and that I was to relate to the members of His family in the same way that I was to relate to Him. The difficulty was that some of them were awkward, some irritating, and some downright obnoxious. However, the interesting thing was that the more I related to them, the more real God became to me. How does that work? Norman Grubb suggested that as you make the effort to relate to others you discover that your relationship with God is widened. You see that God is bigger and grander and greater than you had previously realised. You gain a clearer understanding of Him.

O God, in this delicate, difficult, but delightful business of getting along with other people, help me to gain the skill, insight and patience I need. Amen.

Vertical and horizontal

FOR READING AND MEDITATION
I THESSALONIANS 3:1–13

'May the Lord make your love increase and overflow for each other …' (v.12)

It is my belief that God has so arranged our lives that as we relate to one another in our horizontal relationships, our experience of Him deepens. I have found that the better I relate to others in the Church, the better I relate to God. Human relationships, especially marriage, have brought God closer to me. The greatest way, of course, in which God has demonstrated His love for us was by sending His Son to die for us, as verses such as John 3:16 and Romans 5:8 make plain. But I John 4:12 tells us that God's love is also seen in our love for others – in fact, it is perfected in us. God intends our relationships to be the means by which we give each other a much clearer picture of His own love for us.

Lord God, thank You that You are love. May I experience that love today, and love others with Your love. Amen.

Making God more real to others

FOR READING AND MEDITATION
1 JOHN 4:1–12

'No-one has ever seen God; but if we love one another,
God lives in us and his love is made complete in us.' (v.12)

God is intangible and invisible. We, however, are tangible and visible. We are able to see, touch and hear each other. God doesn't come to you and talk to you in an audible voice or put a warm hand on yours when you are in need of support – but I can. God has made me as a physical being, and He has made you in the same way too. And when I need support, you can give it to me. Together we can make the invisible God more real to each other, and bring about in each other's lives an experiential awareness of what it means to be deeply loved by Him. Seeing this clearly and entering into it fully makes the task of rightly relating to others not a mere duty but a delight.

O God, help me to make You more real to someone today
by tangibly sharing Your love. In Christ's name. Amen.

Sandpaper people

FOR READING AND MEDITATION
PHILIPPIANS 2:1–18

*'Each of you should look not only to your own interests,
but also to the interests of others.' (v.4)*

There are in life what might be termed 'sandpaper people' who rub painfully against us. Their sole ministry, it has been said, is to develop patience in others! Yet God tells us that we are to love them because this is the way in which He loved us and intends us to relate to one another. This old rhyme speaks clearly on the matter: 'To dwell above with saints in love, my, that will be glory. To dwell below with saints we know, now that's a different story.' My bookshelves contain many biographies of saints of the past who allowed God's grace to work in their lives until they overcame such hindrances to their spiritual growth as pettiness, temper and lack of consideration towards others. And we can too.

O Jesus, I long with all my soul to learn the art of loving relationships. I want to think love, feel love and act love, just like You. Amen.

The essence of reality

FOR READING AND MEDITATION
JAMES 2:5–26

'If you really keep the royal law found in Scripture, "Love your neighbour as yourself," you are doing right.' (v.8)

What is the divine purpose behind relationships? It is, I believe, to enable us to understand the essence of reality. D. Broughton Knox says, 'We learn from the Trinity that relationship is of the essence of reality and therefore of the essence of our existence, and we also learn that the way this relationship should be expressed is by concern for others.' I came to see that the energy which pulses at the heart of the Trinity is other-centred. Each member of the Trinity is more concerned about the others than He is about Himself. Movement towards God, I am convinced, involves learning to relate to others in the way the Persons of the Trinity relate to one another – in true other-centredness.

Loving heavenly Father, may I live according to Your design and be more concerned about others than I am about myself. Amen.

The art of loving

FOR READING AND MEDITATION
ROMANS 13:1–10

'Let no debt remain outstanding, except the continuing debt to love one another ...' (v.8)

I used to regard other people as the cause of many of my problems. But then I realised that relationships do not so much cause problems as reveal problems. The problems in my relationships were caused not so much by the way others treated me but by the way I reacted to them. The major problem was not other people, but myself. One of the greatest challenges of my life has been to consider others as more important than myself. Nowhere do I have a greater opportunity to demonstrate other-centredness than in my relationships, in moving in love to those I might even dislike. As we come in contact with people we have an opportunity to practise the art of loving which is of the essence of reality.

Lord, help me to make my relationship with You the strongest relationship in my life and help me practise the art of loving others. Amen.

Living in the light of eternity

FOR READING AND MEDITATION
COLOSSIANS 1:1–7

'… the faith and love that spring from the hope that is stored up for you in heaven …' (v.5)

The fourth aspect of the spiritual journey that we shall consider is *learning to live life in the light of eternity*. Our courage for the journey so often falters because we have lost our hope of heaven – our journey's destination. Take away the hope of arrival in heaven at the end of our journey and our journey becomes no more than a death march. A.J. Conyers sums up the current situation when he says, 'We live in a world no longer under heaven'. Most of the emotional problems we struggle with, he claims, arise from that fact. Much of the rage and deadness that simmers just beneath the surface of our Christian façade has a common root: we live in this world and have no expectation of the world to come.

Gracious Father, wonderful though this world may appear, help me to keep heaven clearly in view. In Christ's name I pray. Amen.

A life without hope?

FOR READING AND MEDITATION
ECCLESIASTES 3:9–22

'He has also set eternity in the hearts of men ...' (v.11)

The philosopher Peter Kreeft believes the crisis of hope that afflicts the Church today is a crisis of imagination. Our images of heaven, he says, are dull, platitudinous and syrupy, therefore so is our faith, our hope and love of heaven. Dullness, not doubt, he claims, is the strongest enemy of our faith, just as indifference, not hate, is the strongest enemy of love. There are so many things that excite me about going to heaven: intimacy, adventure, beauty, joy. In fact heaven is so wonderful that, as Paul writes, '... no mind has conceived what God has prepared for those who love him' (1 Cor. 2:9). And we too will be perfect; in other words, our souls will be what God wanted all along.

Heavenly Father, thank You that I have not been left to my own subjective feelings about heaven. Though I may lose faith in my feelings, I can never lose faith in Your Son. Amen.

Upwards towards heaven

FOR READING AND MEDITATION
HEBREWS 12:1–12

'Let us fix our eyes on Jesus, the author and perfecter of our faith …' (v.2)

The eighteenth-century American theologian, Jonathan Edwards, said, 'This life ought to be spent by us only as a journey towards heaven.' The road stretches ahead of us and our destination awaits us. And that journey will end in unutterable joy. Most of us are fortunate in that we have family and friends who love us, but even they may let us down. When they do, we have several options. We can retreat into cynicism and deaden the pain through self-pity, or we can become demanding and manipulate them into giving us more attention. Or we can remember that the day is coming when we will all live in perfect love. We can let the ache lead us to think more deeply and turn our eyes upwards towards heaven.

Lord Jesus, thank You for making clear to me where my real home is and how I can get there. Help me to keep my eyes fixed on You. Amen.

Forgetting to remember

FOR READING AND MEDITATION
DEUTERONOMY 4:1–14

'... watch yourselves closely so that you do not forget the things your eyes have seen or let them slip from your heart ...' (v.9)

One of the greatest challenges that we face on our journey towards heaven is forgetfulness. The human heart is crippled by forgetfulness. Our memories are short, and we easily forget what we should remember. When I read the story of the golden calf recorded in Exodus 32 I am humbled. How could they be so foolish? How could they forget everything they had received from the hand of God? Dr Martyn Lloyd-Jones commented that we would even forget the Lord's death if it weren't for the reminder provided by the Communion Service. Spiritual amnesia is so likely that, from Genesis to Revelation, the Bible is full of calls to remember.

Father, help me to remember at all times that this world in which I live is just my temporary home because my real home is in heaven. Amen.

Going somewhere?

FOR READING AND MEDITATION
JOHN 13:1–17

'Jesus knew that the time had come for him to leave this world and go to the Father.' (v.1)

How did Jesus sustain His heart in the face of brutal opposition? *He never lost sight of where He was heading.* At the beginning of the story of the washing of the disciples' feet we are told that Jesus knew He had come from God and that He was returning to God. He remembered where He had come from and where He was going. And so must we. We too have come from God and we too are going to Him. It is only as we realise that our time on earth is a journey, and keep our destination in view, that we will truly capture a sense of what this life is all about. You see, my friend, there is an end to this journey, and the end for those who have committed their life to Jesus Christ is both wonderful and glorious.

Father, how exciting it is to be reminded that though I am a loyal member of the country and community in which I live, my real citizenship is in heaven. Amen.

This world is not my home

FOR READING AND MEDITATION
I CORINTHIANS 2:1–16

*'... as it is written: "No eye has seen, no ear has heard ...
what God has prepared for those who love him ..."' (v.9)*

When our eyes are focused on our future in heaven
then one of the consequences is that the material
things which so many crave have little appeal for us. The
Puritan, Thomas Watson, said, 'The world is but a great
inn, where we are to stay a night or two, and be gone;
what madness is it so to set our heart upon our inn as to
forget our home.' Those who keep heaven in view regard
material possessions as no more than the furnishing of
an inn. After all, we are only staying for the night. With
a mind set on God and a heart aflame with supernatural
love, those who move close to God can sing: *This world
is not my home, I'm just a-passing through / My treasures
are laid up somewhere beyond the blue.*

*Gracious and loving heavenly Father, please help me to
keep my eyes fixed on the home You have prepared for me
in heaven. Amen.*

Eyes focused on heaven

FOR READING AND MEDITATION
HEBREWS 9:11–28

*'For Christ did not enter a man-made sanctuary …
he entered heaven itself …' (v.24)*

Heaven is our home; it's where we *belong*. That truth is something we should keep in mind all the time. To talk and think and look forward to heaven is not a sign of an escapist mentality – providing that is not *all* we think about. We work better down here on earth because, by faith, we always have a vision of the perfect end. 'The happiest people on earth,' someone has said, 'are those who keep their eyes focused on heaven.' The psalmist wrote, 'You have made known to me the path of life; you will fill me with joy in your presence, with eternal pleasures at your right hand' (Psa. 16:11). Joy will be found when we get to heaven through realisation, but it can also be found now by anticipation.

O Father, may my eyes be focused on the joys of heaven as I serve You with all my heart here on earth. Amen.

'Inconsolable longings'

FOR READING AND MEDITATION
ISAIAH 55:1–13

*'Why spend money on what is not bread, and your labour
on what does not satisfy?' (v.2)*

Our inner desire for heaven has been described by
C.S. Lewis as 'the inconsolable longing ... news
from a country we have never visited.' If it is true that a
longing for heaven has been built into the human heart,
how does the great mass of humanity go about dealing
with it? One way is to pretend this mysterious aspect of
our existence does not exist. It is a strange fact of life that
this aspect of human nature – the soul's deep sense of
homelessness – is not studied more intently. Perhaps it's
because it fits none of the usual categories of thought. It
can't be labelled, sorted, explained or matched, so men
and women make a detour to avoid it and treat it as if it
wasn't there. But this detour is really a denial.

*My Father and my God, how glad I am that I have found
what my soul truly longs for – You! Amen.*

'Sit quietly before mystery'

FOR READING AND MEDITATION
PSALM 46:1–11

'Be still, and know that I am God …' (v.10)

O ne way people try to face the fact that there is an inconsolable longing in the heart is to reduce it to something explainable. Dr Larry Crabb, a Christian psychologist, says, 'Instead of sitting quietly before mystery, we try to bring it into the area of manageability. What fools we are.' This passion to explain matters is our way of bringing them under our control. We feel less helpless and vulnerable when we are able to manage things than when we have to sit quietly before mystery. But the affairs of the soul cannot always be managed; they are best handled by coming quietly before God in private prayer.

O God, much that is within me is a mystery. But help me to be more concerned with knowing You than knowing myself, for in knowing You I shall better know myself. Amen.

Crisis of confusion

FOR READING AND MEDITATION
PSALM 28:1–9

'The LORD is the strength of his people, a fortress of salvation for his anointed one.' (v.8)

Another topic is that everyone who walks the path of faith will sooner or later come face to face with this issue of *mystery*, which we touched on yesterday. Confusion and mystery, I found as a pastor, are the issues that create such great problems for the people of God. Often people would come to me and say, 'Selwyn, I am so confused by what God is allowing to happen in my life.' They would then tell me all about it, embarking on a story of circumstances that were so perplexing I could see no answer to them. But what brings our Master joy is when we trust Him implicitly even though we have no answers. Some of the answers might not come until the next generation. But be assured – God is at work.

Father, may nothing create distance between You and me because I long for closeness. I am listening, dear Father. Amen.

Exercising muscles of faith

FOR READING AND MEDITATION
PSALM 55:1–23

'Listen to my prayer, O God ... hear me and answer me.'
(vv. 1–2)

Living comfortably with confusion and mystery is not easy. We like to feel we are in control. We like to have answers for everything mysterious because walking in the dark is disturbing. So *any* answer is better than none. Many people will accept glib explanations because it provides them with a way out of confusion. But we fail to see that it is often in the midst of massive confusion that we have the opportunity to build the muscles of faith and trust. The truth is that God has not chosen to answer every question we ask, but He has promised, 'Never will I leave you; never will I forsake you' (Heb. 13:5). Whatever your situation or circumstance, strengthen yourself in God today for He is with you.

O God my Father, even when I am perplexed, may I cling to Your promise to be with me at all times. In Jesus' name. Amen.

My life in God's hands

FOR READING AND MEDITATION
JOB 13:6–24

'Though he slay me, yet will I hope in him; I will surely defend my ways to his face.' (v.15)

Perhaps one of the greatest evidences of our ability to trust is our willingness to walk on in the darkness. Can we trust God? One measure of trust is how deeply we relate to God and are prepared to live without answers. Answers are not essential; trust is. In this world in which we live there are many voices similar to those of Job's so-called friends offering supposed answers and explanations. How deeply do you trust God? A little or a lot? Like Job, in the midst of mystery and confusion we can say, 'I see no sense in this, but I know that God, the Architect of this universe, has my life and times in His hands.' God can be trusted. Take that step of trust today.

Gracious and loving Father, bring me to that place of calm, confident trust in which Job rested. In Jesus' name. Amen.

The Word within

FOR READING AND MEDITATION
JEREMIAH 20:7–13

'O LORD, you deceived me, and I was deceived … I am ridiculed all day long; everyone mocks me.' (v.7)

Reading through the psalms we see the psalmists constantly being overwhelmed by what they cannot control or change. Yet their cry of desperation opens them to the development of a faith and a trust that holds them fast in the midst of everything. And though they do not have answers, they have God. Notice this: God allows us to express our feelings. Jeremiah had allowed God's Word to penetrate his being to such an extent that in the moment of overwhelming test it was the divine Word that cried out the loudest. Similarly, if we allow God's Word to live and take root within us, when our hurts and frustrations scream within, God's Word will burn in us and we too will hear His message above the tumult.

Father, when my emotions scream within me may Your voice be heard above the tumult. This I ask in our Lord's precious name. Amen.

God questions

FOR READING AND MEDITATION
JOB 38:1–20

*'Where were you when I laid the earth's foundation?
Tell me, if you understand.' (v.4)*

S omething happened to Job in this dramatic encounter
with God. It was as if God had said, 'I will not give you
answers, but I will give you something infinitely greater
– I will give you *Myself*.' Job experienced a new revelation
and knowledge of God (42:5). We too, by God's grace,
can walk in the dark knowing that God is good. Mystery
and confusion are part of our spiritual journey, and their
purpose is to increase our trust in God. Though we are
big enough to ask the questions, God knows that we are
not necessarily big enough to understand the answers.
And so, as our confidence in Him increases, we learn to
trust Him even when we cannot trace Him. Our faith
grows stronger and more powerful.

*Father, thank You that in the presence of mystery You do not
necessarily give answers, but You do give Yourself. Amen.*

A change of mind

FOR READING AND MEDITATION
ACTS 2:29–41

'Repent and be baptised, every one of you, in the name of Jesus Christ for the forgiveness of your sins.' (v.38)

Another important step on the journey of faith is *to come to a clear understanding of repentance.* Repentance is not just the way *into* the Christian life, it is much more than that. One of the first things written in Martin Luther's *95 Theses,* is this: 'When our Lord and Master Jesus Christ said "Repent" He willed that the entire life of the believer be one of repentance.' The Greek word for repentance is *metanoia,* which signifies a change of mind. When we become a Christian we repent and change our mind about running our life on our own terms, deciding instead to surrender it to Jesus Christ. That is the initial act of repentance. But this is where many stop instead of start.

Father God, thank You that You have made a way for me to enter into Your presence. To You be the glory. Amen.

Finding our way back

FOR READING AND MEDITATION
REVELATION 2:1–7

'Remember the height from which you have fallen!
Repent and do the things you did at first.' (v.5)

Let's consider how Jesus, the Wonderful Counsellor, deals with the church at Ephesus. He told the Ephesians to remember, repent and *then* return to doing the things they did at first. Often we forget what sin really is. Sin is pushing God out of the place He has reserved for Himself. It's easy to move from dependency on Christ to something else, and when He is no longer first, then in order to restore our relationship with Him we must repent. This, I believe, is something so many forget on the journey of faith. Many believe repentance is a one-off act. But sometimes we seek life in something other than God and we need to repent and change our mind once again about where life is found.

Lord Jesus Christ, please help me to continue finding my life in nothing other than You. Amen.

The first steps of repentance

FOR READING AND MEDITATION
HOSEA 14:1–3

'Return ... to the LORD your God. Your sins have been your downfall!' (v.1)

The teaching on repentance in Hosea shows us a divine pattern to follow. *'Return ... to the LORD your God.'* We have chosen to look elsewhere for the energy to make our lives work; now we must choose to transfer our dependence to God. *'Take words with you ...'*. We must have a clear idea of what we are repenting of, and the clearer our understanding, the deeper our repentance. *'Forgive all our sins ...'*. What is sin? It is the ego in the place God reserved for Himself. We cannot rid ourselves of sin; it has to be forgiven. *'... receive us graciously, that we may offer the fruit of our lips'*. Repentance involves throwing ourselves on the mercy of God so that we may approach Him in true worship.

Gracious Father, Your Word has such clarity and gives me all the directions I need for life. Help me to see the path I should take – and follow it. Amen.

Further steps of repentance

FOR READING AND MEDITATION
HOSEA 14:1–3

'Assyria cannot save us; we will not mount war-horses.'
(v.3)

'Assyria cannot save us; we will not mount war-horses.'
Salvation can only be found in God Himself. *'We will never again say "Our gods" to what our own hands have made'* (v.3). The real issue underlying sin is idolatry, which is choosing to devote ourselves to and trust in something other than the Creator God. Even our foolish attempts to rely on our own strategies as we relate to others are idolatry. *'In you the fatherless find compassion'* (v.3). The willingness to acknowledge our helplessness enables us to see how desperately we need God's love and mercy, and this causes us to turn to Him and become dependent upon Him. When we do, we find He is indeed a compassionate Father.

O God my Father, solemnly and sincerely I take these steps of repentance. I return to the love I had for You at first. Amen.

The benefits of repentance

FOR READING AND MEDITATION
HOSEA 14:4–9

'Who is wise? He will realise these things. Who is discerning? He will understand them.' (v.9)

What happens to those who repent deeply? Firstly, our waywardness is healed (v.4). Our lives become spiritually refreshed. 'I will be like the dew to Israel' (v.5). Our roots go down further into the soil of God's love, giving us a deeper foundation and greater stability (v.5) and we gain an attractiveness that was not there before (v.6). Our new way of living encourages people to want to 'dwell in our shade' (v.7). And finally, we learn that idolatry is futile and that the only fruitfulness that matters is the fruitfulness that comes from submission to God (v.8). When we repent in the way Hosea describes in the first half of this chapter we will experience the benefits he describes in the second half.

Father, remind me of these steps whenever I find myself moving in a direction away from You. In Jesus' name. Amen.

Theology leads to doxology

FOR READING AND MEDITATION
ROMANS 11:11–36

'For from him and through him and to him are all things.
To him be the glory for ever! Amen.' (v.36)

The seventh issue on our transformational journey is the development of a rich devotional life. Many Christians have a good mind and they think a lot; they read the Bible, understand it, believe it, appreciate it, but they lack that heart relationship with the Lord that involves the emotions and the feelings. Like Paul, our theology should lead to doxology or else its purpose is not being fulfilled. Students of theology frequently become immersed in deep theological discussion, but do not always allow it to set their hearts on fire in wonder, love and praise. What our Lord seeks to lead us into is a passionate relationship with Himself. God does not want robotic obedience, but passionate engagement.

My loving heavenly Father, help me come to You now with expectancy. And as I respond to Your great love, may my passion become stronger. Amen.

Passionate engagement with God

FOR READING AND MEDITATION
HOSEA 11:1–12

'My heart is changed within me; all my compassion is aroused.' (v.8)

Hosea, by loving his unfaithful wife, models God's own commitment to His people, and His unfailing love despite their waywardness. God pours out His heart to Israel, promising to take His people back, to heal them and cause them to flourish. God holds that same love for each one of us. He is a passionate Being and He wants to engage with us passionately also. It is so easy for us to be more taken up with the cause of Christ than with Christ Himself, to be preoccupied with the work of God rather than with the God whose work we are called to do. What God longs for more than anything as we travel on this journey is that we have a passionate relationship with Him, and this He desires with all His heart.

O Father, I am grateful for the way in which I have come to know You, but I long to know You still more. Amen.

Where does it begin?

FOR READING AND MEDITATION
1 JOHN 4:7–21

'We love because he first loved us.' (v.19)

Many years ago I told God that I felt that He did not love me enough. In His great kindness He took me to the cross and He gave me a vision which was so wonderful that the scales fell from my eyes and my own love flamed in response. Love for God is not something we can manufacture. Instead, focus on how much He loves you and the Holy Spirit will bring this alive for you. You will begin to grasp what Jesus has done for you. As a consequence, the machinery of your soul will start to turn, and you will begin to love Him back. Our love for God is a response to His love for us. He is a passionate God, continually instigating a relationship with His people.

Father, as I think about how You sent Jesus, Your Son, to this earth to die for us, may the wonder of Your amazing love kindle love in me. Amen.

A beautiful thing

FOR READING AND MEDITATION
MATTHEW 26:1–13

'… *wherever this gospel is preached throughout the world, what she has done will also be told, in memory of her.*' (v.13)

Through my studies I have learned a lot of important things, but it is Mary of Bethany, in her special moment with the Saviour, who has taught me what is most important. In one great extravagant loving act she poured oil over the head of the Lord Jesus. The most important matter is our love relationship with our Lord Jesus Christ. That's what was of significance to Jesus. That's what He called beautiful. That's what He said would be remembered for all time. It is no surprise to me that many commentators have called Mary's anointing of Jesus the loveliest deed of all in the Gospels. It was without doubt a most beautiful act and it brought from the lips of Jesus an unusual and extraordinary commendation.

Lord Jesus, may my relationship with You be one of selfless love. By my actions may I show others just how much I love You. Amen.

Worship first – work second

FOR READING AND MEDITATION
LUKE 10:38–42

'Martha, Martha … Mary has chosen what is better, and it will not be taken away from her.' (vv.41–42)

The Bible college where I trained had this motto: 'Let me never lose the important truth that I must love Thyself more than Thy service.' We can work for God, and He will use our abilities, but more than anything He wants our love. It is a great tragedy that people think of the quiet time, of Bible study and prayer, as being solely about spiritual growth – *our* growth. Our times of devotion are primarily not about us but about God. Activity and intimacy are not mutually exclusive. The point is that our activity for our heavenly Father should grow out of intimacy with Him. Worship first, work second. That is the most effective way to serve Him. We are likely to earn His commendation when everything we do is out of love for Him.

My Father and my Friend, in my times of communion with You may I not present You with a shopping list but instead express my love for You. Amen.

An act of beauty

FOR READING AND MEDITATION
MATTHEW 11:20–30

'Come to me … and I will give you rest.' (v.28)

M ary's anointing of Jesus was an act of beauty that Jesus defended and commended to His disciples. Why does Jesus say this story will be told wherever the gospel is preached? He wants to draw our attention to the fact that the most important thing in our lives is not our grasp of doctrine – though that is essential – but how passionate we are in our love for Him. As far as we know, Mary never cast out devils and never worked miracles, as the disciples did. All she did was love the Saviour. It was the way she loved Him that made the difference – passionately, extravagantly, lavishly. Although there was the scent of perfume, there was so much more – the aroma of extravagant love flowing from Mary's heart.

Father, may my worship be received as the aroma of an extravagant love flowing from my heart. Amen.

Not personal but intimate

FOR READING AND MEDITATION
JOHN 4:1–26

' … *true worshippers will worship the Father in spirit
and truth, for they are the kind of worshippers the Father
seeks.' (v.23)*

As Mary walked away from the cross that same
perfume scent probably still lingered in her hair
– the hair that she used to dry the Saviour's feet (see
John 12:3). It was a reminder of the love that spilled
from His broken body on the cross, the perfume of His
sacrifice that rose to heaven and brought pleasure to the
nostrils of God (Eph. 5:2). So pure, so lovely … so truly
extravagant. It was a sacrifice motivated by love which
He never regretted making, just as I'm sure Mary never
regretted making her own sacrifice prompted by love.
And now, today, as the perfume of our Lord's sacrifice
still fills the air, will you seek to enter into a more
passionate relationship with Him?

*Father, there is in my heart a longing for intimacy, for
beauty, for adventure. The intimacy I enjoy with You now
is, I know, just a foretaste of what is to come. Amen.*

What comes in must go out

FOR READING AND MEDITATION
JOHN 4:27–42

'... the woman ... said to the people, "Come, see a man
who told me everything I ever did."'(vv.28–29)

We now come to the final requirement on our
spiritual journey which brings us closer to God.
On this journey it is essential that we do not simply
take in, absorb and assimilate, but also that we share
– share what we have received from God. So the final
matter is *sharing the faith*. It is important for us to
take time to share with others the things that God has
shared with us. The four words which summarise the
communication of the gospel are 'come ... see ... go
... tell'. We get first-hand knowledge – 'come and see'
– and then the impulse takes over – 'go and tell'. And if
there is no 'go and tell' impulse then perhaps the 'come
and see' impulse is not ours – or has ceased to be a
strong instinct in our lives.

*O Father, I ask not for an experience of You – that I already
have. I ask rather for the courage to share it with others.
Amen.*

'Let me commend my Saviour'

FOR READING AND MEDITATION
MALACHI 3:1–18

'Then those who feared the LORD talked with each other ...'
(v.16)

Experience and expression are the alternate beats of the Christian heart. If these two essentials are not in operation, the Christian heart ceases to beat. Then what happens? We settle down to dead forms, dead attitudes and dead prayers. This matter of sharing must not be limited only to evangelism – it applies also to sharing with other Christians the things that God has shared with us. Nothing is fully ours until we share it – the expression will deepen the impression. So in seeking to stay spiritually fresh, discipline yourself to share appropriate issues with your Christian and non-Christian friends. Someone has defined a Christian as one who says by word or deed, 'Let me commend my Saviour to you'.

Father, may I reach up to You with one hand and reach out to those in need with the other. In Jesus' name. Amen.

Words and deeds

FOR READING AND MEDITATION
I PETER 3:8–22

'Always be prepared to give an answer to everyone who asks you to give the reason for the hope that you have.' (v.15)

Words and deeds are the two wings of the soaring Christian. Those who call for words alone and those who call for deeds alone are both wrong. We belong to Him who had words and deeds in a living blend. Though it is not necessary to constantly preach at people, we must be ready to take advantage of every opportunity to share Christ. Even if we eradicated all poverty and hunger that would still leave people in need of conversion. We must be balanced about this matter, because hungry people may need a meal before they can hear the gospel. Let us not forget, however, that we are commanded to go into the world to preach the gospel (Matt. 28:19–20). That command will never be annulled.

Father, You have committed to us the greatest work in the world – the work of bringing others to You. Help me in Jesus' name. Amen.

Moving towards God

FOR READING AND MEDITATION
2 CORINTHIANS 3:1–18

*'And we, who ... all reflect the Lord's glory, are being
transformed into his likeness with ever-increasing glory ...'*
(v.18)

In summary, during our spiritual journey and
transformation to be like Christ we will encounter
a holy God; through suffering, our sensitivity to the
needs of others is deepened and widened. In close
relationships we learn the art of loving others more
than we love ourselves. We live in the light of eternity
and with mystery, trusting in God. Our lives are
characterised by repentance as we continuously return
to Him and we rejoice that throughout our journey we
are accompanied by a passionate God who desires an
intimate, vibrant relationship with us. Lastly we share
what God has so graciously shared with us. Well, there
it is – the irreducible minimum of what I believe is vital
for movement towards God.

*Lord Jesus Christ, help us to love You the way Mary of
Bethany did, and may we be as devoted to You as she was.
Amen.*

Shut up – to write

FOR READING AND MEDITATION
COLOSSIANS 1:1

'Paul, an apostle of Christ Jesus by the will of God ...' (v.1)

For the next two months we shall study Paul's letter to the Colossians. This was probably written by him during his imprisonment in Rome in AD 62 or 63. Paul begins by outlining his credentials: 'an apostle of Christ Jesus by the will of God'. Our first reaction might be to think it sad that an apostle should be shut up in prison rather than winning new territories for Christ. But although circumstances prevented him from travelling, his spirit was free to reach out through his pen. Had he not been imprisoned we would not have had the captivity letters – Colossians, Ephesians, Philippians and Philemon. From prison his influence extended to the ends of the earth and throughout the ages. He was shut up – to write.

O Father, physical restrictions may hinder me bodily but my spirit is always free to soar. Circumstances do not have the last word in my life – You do. Amen.

'Grace and peace'

FOR READING AND MEDITATION
COLOSSIANS 1:2

*'To the holy and faithful brothers in Christ at Colosse:
Grace and peace to you from God our Father.' (v.2)*

Paul writes, 'Grace and peace to you from God our Father.' Notice the words: *'from God our Father'*. Can grace and peace come from sources other than the Father? Of course. 'Grace' and 'peace' are words often used by non-Christians. Mortgage lenders talk about periods of 'grace'; politicians talk about negotiating 'peace' between warring countries. But what a difference between the grace and peace stemming from human hearts and the grace and peace that come from the heart of the Father. One is temporal, the other eternal; one limited, the other unlimited. The best of men and women are only men and women at best. But what comes from God is always perfect. *Perfect* peace, *perfect* grace.

*Father, when the peace and grace You give flow into my
life then I need never be impoverished. Your heart is always
open to give; may my heart be always open to receive. In
Jesus' name. Amen.*

Scripture's Siamese twins

FOR READING AND MEDITATION
COLOSSIANS 1:3–4

'We always thank God … because we have heard of your faith … and of the love you have …' (vv.3–4)

How encouraging for the Colossians to know they were remembered in Paul's prayers. He had heard good things about them from Epaphras (v.7), and so, whenever he prayed for them, he gave thanks to God for their faith in Christ and their love for all their fellow believers. These words link two important qualities: faith and love. The New Testament often joins these two together; sometimes they are even called 'Scripture's Siamese twins'. If you are to have enduring, selfless love for others you must first of all have faith in God. Without a relationship with God, love for others soon runs out of impetus and energy. Governments can raise people's standard of living but they can't love them. Only when we have faith in God can we go on loving the unlovely and the unresponsive. No faith in God, no love like God's.

O God my Father, teach me the secret of faith and love, the alternate beats of the Christian heart. Amen.

A spring in our step

FOR READING AND MEDITATION
COLOSSIANS 1:5

'... the faith and love that spring from the hope that is
stored up for you in heaven ...' (v.5)

Paul tells us faith and love come from the *hope* that
is stored up for us in heaven. It is important to
remember that the Christian experience is characterised
by hope as much as by faith and love. Christian hope
is as certain, if not more certain, as tomorrow's dawn.
It is the assurance that however much we enjoy God's
presence and blessings here on earth, we will experience
something far, far greater in heaven. Notice, too, that
hope is not a consequence of faith and love but its origin.
Faith and love *spring* from hope. When we hold before us
the sure and certain hope of eternal bliss in heaven then
out of that hope spring faith and love. They don't just
saunter into our lives – they *spring*!

*O God, help me keep the prospect of heaven always in
mind. Then I know faith and love will 'spring'. Amen.*

'That's the truth'

FOR READING AND MEDITATION
COLOSSIANS 1:5-6

'All over the world this gospel is bearing fruit and growing ...' (v.6)

How we need in this postmodern age, when people are claiming that what is true for one person may not be true for another, to grasp what Francis Schaeffer described as 'true truth'. 'True truth' is the truth contained in the gospel of Jesus Christ. It is the final truth. Nothing can be added to it or subtracted from it. It is the truth, the whole truth and nothing but the truth. Sometimes I find when talking to young adults about Christ, they adopt the attitude, 'Well, that may be true for you, but I have a different truth.' The truth of the gospel, however, is not relative (one thing for me and another thing for you); it is absolute and therefore universal – the same truth for all. That's the truth.

Father, how grateful I am for the simplicity of the gospel. It is the true truth. May I never be moved from its simplicity. Amen.

High praise indeed

FOR READING AND MEDITATION
COLOSSIANS 1:7-8

'You learned it from Epaphras, our dear fellow-servant, who is a faithful minister of Christ ...' (v.7)

E paphras was the founder of the church at Colosse and 'our dear fellow-servant, who is a faithful minister'. This is high praise indeed. Some say that the final test of an individual's work is not only to ask, 'What has he or she done?' but also, 'Could other people work with them?' Epaphras was such a person – a good co-worker. Yet, in addition, he was a 'faithful minister'. He wasn't merely loyal to his fellow-workers in the ministry; he devoted himself to the needs of those he served. Paul continues, 'who also told us of your love in the Spirit'. Epaphras would have been well aware of the faults of the Colossian Christians, but he was not obsessed by them and praised what could be praised.

O God, may I be easy to work with, devoted to Jesus Christ, and see the good in others more readily than the bad. Amen.

There's more

FOR READING AND MEDITATION
COLOSSIANS 1:9–10

*'… we have not stopped praying for you and asking God
to fill you with the knowledge of his will …' (v.9)*

After telling the Colossian Christians that he had
prayed ceaselessly for them since the day he had
heard about them, Paul makes the first of his petitions
by asking God to fill them 'with the knowledge of his
will through all spiritual wisdom and understanding'.
Notice the word 'fill'. It suggests that however much the
Colossian Christians had received from the Lord, there
was still room for more. You see, no one can ever rest
and say, 'I am now *completely* Christian'. For the Holy
Spirit always has more to teach us about the will of God.
Rabindranath Tagore, the Indian poet, said, 'The eternal
cry is – more'. Whatever the Colossians knew of God,
there was much more to discover.

*O God, there is always room in my heart for more
understanding of Your will. And the more I receive, the
more I long for. Amen.*

You'll get through

FOR READING AND MEDITATION
COLOSSIANS 1:11–12

'… being strengthened with all power … so that you may have great endurance and patience …' (v.11)

There's nothing wrong with asking God for His power to save, heal and deliver. But what Paul has in mind as he prays for power is a power to endure all trials and come through them with thanksgiving. Today many of you contend with fierce antagonism, bitter disappointment, rejection from friends or family, a financial reversal and so on. But listen carefully: *you will get through.* And the reason you will get through is because God's power is at work in your life. You may be shaken but you will not be shattered, knocked down but not knocked out. What is more, you will come through the experience with thanksgiving. You will be thankful because through your difficulties you will be brought closer to God Himself.

Father, You do not promise to keep me from difficulties, but You do promise me that You will bring me through. On that I can rely. Amen.

Gone! Gone!

FOR READING AND MEDITATION
COLOSSIANS 1:12–14

'... the Father ... has qualified you to share in the
inheritance of the saints ...' (v.12)

All the conditions necessary for becoming an heir
of God and a joint heir with Christ had been met
by the Colossians' acceptance of Christ, and they were
now full members of God's new society . But more: they
had been 'rescued', and in Christ 'we have redemption,
the forgiveness of sins'. The Christian faith begins at the
point of redemption. We need redemption from sin –
release from the bondage of sin – and forgiveness for our
sins. Both are provided in Jesus Christ. I know of nothing
more wonderful than redemption and forgiveness. The
slate is wiped clean. Once I ask for forgiveness from
Christ then I am, as far as God is concerned, a person
without a past history. I am just like a newborn baby; I
have a future but no past. How amazing.

*O Father, help me open my heart to the thrilling fact that all
my sins are gone. Gone! Hallelujah!*

The right way for everything

FOR READING AND MEDITATION
COLOSSIANS 1:15–16

'He is the image of the invisible God, the firstborn over all creation.' (v.15)

If everything is created *by* Christ and *for* Christ then creation is designed to work His way. When it does it works effectively; when it follows some other way it works towards its ruin. What is being said is this: the way of Christ is written not only into the texts of Scripture but into the texture of the whole of creation. If we are created by Christ and for Christ then He is inescapable. Just as you cannot jump out of your skin so you cannot escape Christ, for His stamp is upon the whole of His creation. Like the watermark in paper, Christ is written into the structure of our beings. This means that Christ's way is the right way to do everything, and all other ways are the wrong way.

Father, I am so thankful I know You, but I pray for revival that many others may come to know You too. Amen.

Christ – a centripetal force

FOR READING AND MEDITATION
COLOSSIANS 1:17–18

'He is before all things, and in him all things hold together.' (v.17)

These words clinch everything: 'in him all things hold together'. We could also say, 'Out of Him all things fly apart – they go to pieces'. One commentator said: 'Everything in Him [Jesus] is centripetal; everything outside of Him is centrifugal.' Everything in Christ is bound together in perfect harmony, not simply by power but by love. Later in Colossians we read: 'And over all these virtues put on love, which binds them all together in perfect unity' (3:14). Jesus said, 'He who is not with me is against me, and he who does not gather with me scatters' (Matt. 12:30). Everything outside of Christ scatters. Get among any group of Christians, talk about Christ, and you are together. Talk about our church traditions and you are apart.

O Father, I am so grateful that Your Son is my centre and my circumference. In Him I am held together. In Jesus' name. Amen.

'The Order of the Resurrection'

FOR READING AND MEDITATION
COLOSSIANS 1:18

'And he is the head of the body, the church …' (v.18)

Colossians and Ephesians have similar themes, but looked at from different perspectives. Ephesians can be described as the letter which portrays the Church of Christ, whereas Colossians depicts the Christ of the Church. Ephesians focuses on the Body; Colossians focuses on the Head. What does Paul mean when he says Christ 'is the beginning and the firstborn from among the dead'? He is referring, of course, to our Lord's resurrection. Christ's rising from the dead marked the beginning of a new order – what might be called 'The Order of the Resurrection'. Others who were physically raised from the dead were raised only to die again. Those who die in Christ will be raised *never* to die again.

Father, how glad I am that I belong to 'The Order of the Resurrection'. All honour and glory be to Your wonderful name. Amen.

Christ – the pleasure of God

FOR READING AND MEDITATION
COLOSSIANS 1:19–20

'For God was pleased to have all his fulness dwell in him ...' (v.19)

Jesus' divinity is part of His nature. The very essence of God resides in Him. In Him the supernatural is natural. When I consider the sinless life of Jesus, it is no surprise that at the River Jordan God opened the heavens and declared, 'This is my Son, whom I love; with him *I am well pleased*' (Matt. 3:17). No wonder, for He is such a wonderful Son. Paul also reminds us that Jesus is the One who effects reconciliation for all things. When Christ sacrificed His life on the cross, He took on Himself the curse of sin. The cross makes peace possible in every corner of the universe. Christ restores to the universe the principle of harmony which sin so brutally disturbed.

Father, how I long to be an agent of reconciliation and show others how to be at peace with You through Christ. Amen.

Three life positions

FOR READING AND MEDITATION
COLOSSIANS 1:21–23

'Once you were alienated from God and were enemies in your minds …' (v.21)

P aul reminds the Colossians of what Christ has done. Indeed, we should never tire of hearing it, for the central dynamic of the Christian life is not what we do for Christ, but what He has done for us. Dick Lucas gives a good analysis of these verses when he divides them as follows: what you once were, where you now stand, and how you must go on. And what were we? 'Enemies,' says Paul. Yet where are we now through grace? Reconciled. The enmity is over and peace has come to our hearts. We stand in God's presence 'holy … without blemish and free from accusation'. And how should we go on? We are to 'continue in [the] faith, established and firm, not moved from the hope held out in the gospel' (v.23).

Father, grant that I might never move away from the gospel that challenged me and changed me. In Jesus' name I pray. Amen.

The continuing cross

FOR READING AND MEDITATION
COLOSSIANS 1:24

'… I fill up in my flesh what is still lacking in regard to Christ's afflictions …' (v.24)

When Paul says he must fill up in his flesh 'what is still lacking in regard to Christ's afflictions' is he suggesting there was some deficiency in Christ's atonement? No: Christ had suffered on the cross for the sins of the world and now Paul 'filled up Christ's afflictions by experiencing the added sufferings necessary to carry this good news to a lost world' (NIV Study Bible). Paul is saying something like this: 'Daily I enter into the crucifixion of Jesus, take my share of His sufferings, and bleed with Him and for Him. I am in Christ, therefore I participate in His sufferings for the Church.' Next time you have a cross to bear because of some people remember Christ bore a cross for all the people.

Father, I accept that because I am in Christ I am involved in His sufferings also. Help me to regard this as a real privilege and not a burden. Amen.

Saying goodbye to a text

FOR READING AND MEDITATION
COLOSSIANS 1:25

'I have become its servant by the commission God gave me to present to you the word of God in its fulness ...' (v.25)

What constitutes a God-given ministry? *Having the heart of a servant.* There are many definitions of servanthood, but the one I most like is: 'becoming excited about making other people successful.' True servanthood will always involve a desire to make the Word of God fully known and Christians fully mature. A man once said to me, 'Our pastor always begins with a text from the Bible ... then immediately says goodbye to it.' A text taken out of context quickly becomes a pretext. Though there is a place for topical preaching, if a church does not have a regular system of presenting to its people a comprehensive exposition of the Scriptures, then the Word of God will not be fully known or will be misunderstood.

Father, I see that only through systematic study of Your Word can it be fully understood. Help all Your servants handle the Word of God well. Amen.

A Christ not in us ...

FOR READING AND MEDITATION
COLOSSIANS 1:26–27

'... the glorious riches of this mystery, which is Christ in you, the hope of glory.' (v.27)

Focus with me now on the phrase 'Christ in you, the hope of glory'. There are many who accept that Christ is for them, but they have no experience of Christ being in them. They may be ready to assert with the rest of us that we have an advocate with the Father, Jesus Christ, the Righteous One (1 John 2:1), but they do not know Him as a power within them. Paul is saying the secret of maturity is having Christ within – thinking, willing and feeling in the heart of His consenting servant. To have Christ near to us is not enough. He must be *in* us, subduing the deep selfishness of our nature, ridding us of our moral rottenness. And as William Law said, 'A Christ not in us is ... a Christ not ours.'

O Father, what a thought: Christ is not just near to me or around me but living in me. How wonderful. Amen.

Beyond 'small talk'

FOR READING AND MEDITATION
COLOSSIANS 1:28

'We proclaim him, admonishing and teaching everyone with all wisdom …' (v.28)

I am sure Paul enjoyed 'small talk' in the same way that we do, but I am sure also that when he saw a need to correct, encourage, or exhort, he would immediately seize the opportunity to do so. Paul concentrated on the goal of bringing others to maturity, and I can imagine him asking at appropriate times questions such as these of his fellow believers: How is your prayer life going? What's your relationship with the Lord like? Are you having any struggles that you might want me to pray about or help you with? How different relationships would be in the Body of Christ if, when talking with our Christian brothers and sisters, we were as interested in their spiritual health as we are in their physical health.

Father, may I become excited about encouraging others to grow spiritually. I yield my all to be mature and to help others become mature. Amen.

'Superhuman energy'

FOR READING AND MEDITATION
COLOSSIANS 1:29

*'To this end I labour, struggling with all his energy, which
so powerfully works in me.' (v.29)*

The words, 'To this end I labour' sound strained and
tense, but then we come to the next part of the
verse, 'struggling with all his energy, which so powerfully
works in me'. The Amplified Version expresses it like
this: 'For this I labour, striving with all the superhuman
energy which He so mightily enkindles and works within
me.' Paul's labour did not depend on human energy but
the power that came from Christ. He lived using all the
energy Christ generated within him. Paul put into his
ministry all the energy he could muster, and found that
as he did, Christ added His energy also. He poured out
what was poured in, not with reservation but with *all*
the energy which Christ generated within him.

*O God, help me experience the energy of Christ working in
me and through me. In His name I pray. Amen.*

One heart and one mind

FOR READING AND MEDITATION
COLOSSIANS 2:1–2

'My purpose is that they may be encouraged in heart and united in love ...' (v.2)

Paul is concerned about error and aware that lasting unity depends on truth as well as love. The believers at Colosse need to be of one mind as well as one heart. The false teachers in Colosse believed that revelation could be received outside of the Saviour, but here Paul lays down the thought that all essential truth is found *in* Christ, and they need not look any further than Him for spiritual understanding. The unity of believers is at risk when the people of God are not of one mind on the things that are *essential*. A common mind about the truths of the Bible and the supremacy of Christ is the only possible basis for Christian unity. If there is not one mind there cannot be one heart.

O Father, help Your children everywhere to have not only one heart but also one mind. In Jesus' name we pray. Amen.

A meditation on the cross

FOR READING AND MEDITATION
MATTHEW 27:32–56

'About the ninth hour Jesus cried out … "My God, my God, why have you forsaken me?"' (v.46)

L et's pause to reflect on the cross and the open tomb. Three thoughts form the basis of my meditations. First, *apart from the cross I would never realise the enormity of my sin*. How terrible my sins must be to a holy God if the only way He could expunge them was to allow His Son to die for me. Second, *apart from the cross I would have no clear focus for my faith*. Whenever a doubt arises in my mind concerning God's love, I stand at the foot of the cross where it is quickly laid to rest. A God who loved me enough to send His Son to die for me has got to be Love. Third, *apart from the cross I would not have a Saviour*. The cross shows me that Jesus Christ has done everything required for my salvation.

Father I thank You that You do not love me because Christ died, but Christ died because You love me. I am loved, lifted and loosed. Amen.

In the spirit He waits

FOR READING AND MEDITATION
LUKE 23:44–56

'The women … followed Joseph and saw the tomb and how his body was laid in it.' (v.55)

How calm and private the tomb was after the shameful public spectacle of the crucifixion. How quiet and still! Do you think of a tomb as being cold and eerie? Not this one. It was filled with destiny. Step inside with me for a moment. Our crucified Saviour lies there on a cool bed of rock. In the spirit He waits. What is He waiting for? To fulfil prophecy, to reverse the human verdict passed on Him, to prove that He really died on the cross and did not just swoon, to validate the victory won on the cross. There are many reasons. He waits and waits and waits. And then, to quote Alice Meynell: *All alone, alone, alone, He rose again behind the stone.*

O Father, I never tire of hearing the story of my Lord's death and resurrection. It is the most glorious thing that has ever happened. Amen.

'The New Year's Day'

FOR READING AND MEDITATION
JOHN 20:1–18

'Then Simon Peter ... saw the strips of linen lying there, as well as the burial cloth ...' (vv.6–7)

Let us stand once again at the open tomb and reflect on what happened there. When Jesus came back from the dead He did not quietly and laboriously unwind strips of linen used as grave clothes. This was not an unwinding, this was a glorious uprising! The very concept of resurrection is supernatural. The natural process of physical decomposition was not arrested or reversed but superseded. Peter and John were the first to see the evidence of the most sensational thing that has ever happened on this planet. As John Stott puts it, 'We live and die; Christ died and lives.' And because He lives we live also. No wonder A.B. Simpson described Easter as 'The New Year's Day of the soul'.

Lord Jesus Christ, now, because You live, I live also. All honour and glory be to Your wonderful name. Amen.

An exciting treasure hunt

FOR READING AND MEDITATION
COLOSSIANS 2:3

'… in whom are hidden all the treasures of wisdom and knowledge.' (v.3)

The point Paul has been making is that no essential truths are withheld from anyone who belongs to Jesus Christ. 'All' – notice the 'all'– '*all* the treasures of wisdom and knowledge' are hidden in Him. But notice also that the truth is hidden. That means our Lord conceals as well as reveals. You know and you don't know; you see and you don't see. But what you don't know and don't see spurs you on to an exciting treasure hunt of further discovery in the Scriptures. 'This unfolding revelation of Christ,' says one writer, 'puts a surprise around every corner, makes life pop with novelty and discovery, makes life well worth the living.' The Christian life is dynamic, not static.

O Father, I am on the most exciting treasure hunt in the world – set to discover the treasures hidden in Christ. Amen.

'In good order'

FOR READING AND MEDITATION
COLOSSIANS 2:4–5

'I tell you this so that no-one may deceive you by fine-sounding arguments.' (v.4)

Though error was threatening the churches at Colosse and Laodicea, it is obvious from Paul's next words that not everything was bad. 'I ... delight to see how orderly you are and how firm your faith in Christ is.' These two go together – orderliness and a firm faith in Christ. It works the other way also: where there is no firmness of faith in Christ there is no order; instead there is disorder. Firmness of faith in Christ and good order are root and fruit. Loss of faith in Christ and disorder are also root and fruit. In Him we are in good order; out of Him we are in disorder.

Father, I am so thankful that life holds together at the centre when our faith is fixed firmly in Your Son. We stay in good order when we are under Your orders. Amen.

Give, take, build

FOR READING AND MEDITATION
COLOSSIANS 2:6–7

'... just as you received Christ Jesus as Lord, continue to live in him ...' (v.6)

No better definition of the essentials of the Christian life could be given than this: 'as you received Christ Jesus as Lord, continue to live in him'. These two requirements – receiving and continuing – should be made clear to every new Christian. Some think receiving Christ is the end, but it is only the beginning. Established in Him we are built up in Him. The foundation is there to be built on. How did we receive Christ? By surrender and receptivity. We give to Him and take from Him. Our giving involves giving the one and only thing we own – ourselves. When He has that, He has all. And part of the purpose of giving is so that we may receive. God asks that we give our all in order that He may give His all.

Dear Father, let all I take from You enable me to give more and build more. I long to be the best I can be for You. Amen.

Godless philosophies

FOR READING AND MEDITATION
COLOSSIANS 2:8

*'See to it that no-one takes you captive through hollow
and deceptive philosophy ...' (v.8)*

J.B. Phillips words Paul's cautionary message like this:
'Be careful that nobody spoils your faith through
intellectualism or high-sounding nonsense. Such stuff
is at best founded on men's ideas of the nature of the
world and disregards Christ!' Philosophy is defined by
the dictionary as 'seeking after wisdom or knowledge,
especially that which deals with ultimate reality'. Yet
any philosophy that is not built on God's revelation in
Scripture leads nowhere. It would appear false teachers
were attempting to persuade believers that Christ was
not God's final revelation and that they could gain a
deeper experience of salvation through enlightenment.
But our Lord is the *truth*, as well as the way and the life.

*Gracious and loving heavenly Father, how glad I am that
my faith has come to rest in Christ and in Him alone.
Amen.*

'Music vaster than before'

FOR READING AND MEDITATION
COLOSSIANS 2:9

'For in Christ all the fulness of the Deity lives in bodily form ...' (v.9)

J ust in case some might claim God came into matter temporarily and partially, Paul says that *'all the fulness of the Deity* lives in bodily form'. There is nothing in God that isn't in Jesus – at least in character and essence. Jesus is God accommodated to human form, not for a short time, but now and always. Christ's body was taken up into heaven and will probably bear the marks of the nail prints through all eternity. His humanity is not something He takes off like a wrap. Christ is both human and divine – for ever. In our Lord body and spirit were reconciled, and because of that, as one poet put it, 'There beats out music vaster than before'.

O Lord Jesus Christ, the meeting place of God and man, matter and spirit, I worship you. Amen.

'Fulness of life in Christ'

FOR READING AND MEDITATION
COLOSSIANS 2:10

'… and you have been given fulness in Christ, who is the Head over every power and authority.' (v.10)

We ourselves have been given fulness in Christ. The false teachers, who regarded the material body as evil, had bypassed the incarnation, saying it was beneath God's dignity to touch matter, let alone enter into it. Instead they taught you could attain fulness of life by knowing God directly. In reality, however, we come to fulness of life in Jesus Christ or we do not come to it at all. Let me pick up Jesus' famous statement once again: 'I am the way and the truth *and the life*' (John 14:6, my emphasis). He is life, and He alone gives us fulness of life – when we are united with Him we share in the very nature of God and the victory Christ has won.

O God, help me to make this my affirmation: in Christ there is fulness of life; outside of Him there is emptiness of life. Amen.

Complete in Him

FOR READING AND MEDITATION
COLOSSIANS 2:11–12

'In him you were also circumcised, in the putting off of the sinful nature ...' (v.11)

False teachers seem to have been combining the Gentile idea of salvation through enlightenment, with the Jewish tradition of circumcision, dietary rules, and religious festivals. Paul says that circumcision is unnecessary because they already possess a purification of which Christ is the source. In verse 10 he makes the point that Christians are spiritually complete in Christ. Here he adds the thought that we are complete in Christ only when we acknowledge His completeness – when we demonstrate our faith in Him. 'It takes a complete Christ,' said D.L. Moody, 'to make a complete Christian.' It's no good saying Christ is complete then trying to add something to Him. He is either complete or incomplete. Period.

O Father, I see the importance of trusting only in You and in the atoning merits of Your Son for my salvation. Amen.

Our cancelled IOUs

FOR READING AND MEDITATION
COLOSSIANS 2:13–14

'He forgave us all our sins, having cancelled the written code ... nailing it to the cross.' (vv.13–14)

'Written code' means a handwritten note. It is the Greek term for an IOU – an acknowledgement of a debt. The word translated 'cancelled' means to sponge or wipe off. This is what Christ has done with our sins. The written code that condemned us has been sponged off by the blood of Christ. It is as if it had never been. Paul then says, 'he took it away, nailing it to the cross'. In ancient times the record of a debt, after it had been paid, would sometimes be nailed to a public notice board so that everyone could see the matter was settled. Our Lord has taken the debt we owed and nailed it to the most public place in the universe – the cross. Jesus cried out, 'It is finished' (John 19:30).

Father, when the hosts of hell try to tell me that my sins are not forgiven I shall point them to the cross and show them the cancelled note. Amen.

Stripped of sham authority

FOR READING AND MEDITATION
COLOSSIANS 2:15

'And having disarmed the powers and authorities, he made a public spectacle of them ...' (v.15)

There is little doubt that the picture Paul had in mind was that of the triumphal procession that customarily took place after a great conquest in Roman times. Hundreds of weary prisoners of war would be tied to chariots and dragged through the streets so that everyone could witness their misery and shame. For the citizens who belonged to the conquering army it was a wonderful sight, but a terrible and humiliating experience for those who had been conquered. Just as the Roman citizens could see that they had nothing to fear from the once proud soldiers now defeated and being paraded before them, so we no longer need to fear Satan and his minions. The cross proclaims Christ's victory, not His defeat!

O Father, I see that Christ's victory on the cross is my victory too. He won it by fighting; I enter into it by just trusting. It sounds too good to be true. But also too good not to be true. Amen.

Shadow-lands

FOR READING AND MEDITATION
COLOSSIANS 2:16–17

'Therefore do not let anyone judge you by what you eat or drink, or with regard to a religious festival ...' (v.16)

Paul encourages the Colossian believers to celebrate Christ's victory for them in a life free from unnecessary rituals and ceremonies. He says, 'These are a shadow of the things that were to come; the reality, however, is found in Christ.' The shadow-land referred to here is the law found in the Old Testament. The rituals it prescribed were to be kept, but they were just *shadows* of what was to come. Their true value lay not in what they were but what they pointed to. Christ is the fulfilment of all that the Old Testament prefigured, and in Him is found all spiritual reality. Those who depend on rituals and ceremonies for their salvation are living in the shadows. Christ is all that is needed. All.

Father, how glad I am that I am in Christ and He is in me. What need have I of standing in the shadows when I can stand in the sunshine of Your love? Amen.

Pride must die ...

FOR READING AND MEDITATION
COLOSSIANS 2:18

'Do not let anyone who delights in false humility and the worship of angels disqualify you for the prize.' (v.18)

S ome commentators believe one aspect of the heresy threatening the church at Colosse was the veneration of angels – the idea being to seek out mediators in addition to Christ. Paul has no intention of allowing the false teaching to rob those who are 'in Christ' of their prize, and characterises the individuals concerned: 'Such a person goes into great detail about what he has seen [in visions], and his unspiritual mind puffs him up with idle notions.' Here we see the root of the trouble: those advocating the worship of angels were puffed up with pride. They claimed to have inside knowledge but really they had found a 'spiritual' way (so called) of drawing attention to themselves instead of Christ.

Father, help me remember that it was pride that turned an angel into the devil and brought havoc to this fair universe. Amen.

Keep connected

FOR READING AND MEDITATION
COLOSSIANS 2:19

'He has lost connection with the Head, from whom the whole body ... grows ...' (v.19)

Paul gives us another reason for the problems at Colosse: the type of person causing trouble had lost connection with the Head. Apparently they were still part of the congregation, but had not held fast to Christ, the Head of the Church. Paul shows us in this verse that when we drift away from Christ then we also drift away from each other. Show me a church where the members have lost connection with the Head and I will show you a church whose members have lost connection with each other. That church may have exciting community projects, a wonderful musical programme and clever debates, but if its members are not united with Christ then it no longer functions as a church; it becomes a club.

Father, I see that growth comes only when we, Your people, are connected to the Head. Help us stay connected, dear Father. Amen.

Rules versus relationships

FOR READING AND MEDITATION
COLOSSIANS 2:20–22

'Since you died with Christ to the basic principles of this world, why ... do you submit to its rules ...?' (v.20)

It is obvious that the world cannot do without religion since humanity, having been made in God's image, has an inbuilt desire to worship. Since it rejects Christ as the only way to God, it has to find the elements of its religious structure elsewhere. Satan, the prince of this world, delights in providing people with a religion of rules and regulations that satisfies their need to worship but does not ask them to bow the knee to Christ. Since you died with Christ, says Paul, you are not governed by rules, but by your relationship with Him. You are saved not by what You do but by what Christ has done. God has put the Church in the world, but we must make sure that the world does not get into the Church.

Father, thank You I am not governed by rules but live freely in relationship with You because of Christ. Amen.

The problem of the self

FOR READING AND MEDITATION
COLOSSIANS 2:23

'Such regulations ... have an appearance of wisdom, with their self-imposed worship, their false humility ...' (v.23)

Wwe must pause for a moment to make clear what is meant by 'self-imposed worship'. J.B. Phillips translates this phrase as 'self-inspired efforts at worship'. The people Paul is denouncing worshipped God not in the way He wants to be worshipped but in the way they *thought* He should be worshipped. They were using supposedly spiritual practices as a means to pander to their self-centredness and pride in their own efforts. In my opinion, self-centredness lies at the root of most of our spiritual problems. If we could eliminate self-centredness from the human heart we would have very few difficulties. Of that I am sure. And self-centredness is never more deadly than when it is dressed up as spirituality.

Gracious and loving heavenly Father, may I not use my faith in the service of self-centredness and egotism. In Jesus' name. Amen.

Our chief business

FOR READING AND MEDITATION
COLOSSIANS 3:1

'Since ... you have been raised with Christ, set your hearts on things above ...' (v.1)

The first half of Colossians is doctrinal and the second practical. Living for Christ is Paul's theme as he begins this third chapter, and he deals with it in terms of *relationships*. First, our relationship with Christ, second, relationships in the local church, third, relationships with the family, fourth, relationship to one's daily work, and fifth, relationships with unbelievers. It has been said that 'The chief business of every Christian is to maintain his relationship with Christ'. If this relationship is not kept intact then it is impossible for other relationships to succeed. A Christian is someone who, in a sense, lives in two places at once: in their earthly residence and in Christ.

Father, in coming to Jesus I have come home. Please help me to be at home in Him – even more at home than I am in my own home. Amen.

At home in the heavenly realm

FOR READING AND MEDITATION
COLOSSIANS 3:2–3

'For you died, and your life is now hidden with Christ in God.' (v.3)

Unlike some other world religions, the Christian faith has no geographical centre. Judaism focuses on Jerusalem and Islam on Mecca. The Christian faith, however, focuses on heaven, where Christ is seated at the right hand of God. Without being 'other worldly' and ignoring our responsibilities here on earth, we seek the things that are beyond the earth. We have died in Christ and now we enjoy a new life – a life that is hidden with Christ in God. A wise old Christian was once asked by another believer, 'Where do you live?' With a twinkle in his eye he passed on his business card to the enquirer and said, 'This is where my residence is, but if you really want to know where I live – I live *in Christ*.'

O God my Father, help me to be at home in the heavenly realm. In Jesus' name. Amen.

What a day that will be!

FOR READING AND MEDITATION
COLOSSIANS 3:4

'When Christ, who is your life, appears, then you also will appear with him in glory.' (v.4)

Here the thought which Paul has been developing through the first verses of this chapter is brought to completion. The day will dawn when the Christ, whom we worship but do not see, will be revealed to the world in all His glory. If we were to paraphrase this verse it would read something like this: 'When Christ, your real life, shows Himself physically and visibly once again in the world, you, who are His people, will be as glorious as He.' What a day that will be! When Christ returns it will not just be that His glory is manifested; it will be glory for me also. And for you, if you belong to Him.

Dear Lord, the promise that I will be with You in glory is what keeps me going. What a day that will be! Come, Lord Jesus. Amen.

An idol factory

FOR READING AND MEDITATION
COLOSSIANS 3:5–6

*'Put to death, therefore, whatever belongs to your earthly
nature …' (v.5)*

Setting our hearts on the things that are above, and
searching our hearts for those things that hinder
Christ's life from flowing through us, go together. Even
though we are Christians and have been saved from
the power of sin, that does not mean that the roots of
sin have been dislodged from our hearts and will never
trouble us again. Even after decades of following Christ
and being conscious of His Spirit at work in my life, I
am aware that my heart has the possibility of becoming
an idol factory. That's why, in addition to setting my
affections on things above, I must also search my heart.
The one follows on from the other.

*Father, I ask for Your divine illumination as I search my
heart. And whatever I find there that is displeasing to You,
help me to put it to death. Amen.*

'I'm in for it now'

FOR READING AND MEDITATION
COLOSSIANS 3:6–7

'Because of these, the wrath of God is coming.' (v.6)

Paul is talking here, of course, not about those who sin and then confess their sin, but those who continue in sin. Those who sin and cry out to God in repentance are at once forgiven and restored. But let's face it, often God does not seem in a hurry to judge. How many times have believers committed sin, not repented, and said to themselves, 'I'm in for it now' but seemingly nothing has happened? The truth is that God's judgments are often silent – something dies within us when we continue in sin. We become less of a person. Our creativity shrivels up, our zest for life is eroded by guilt, our ability to stand stress is reduced. The worst thing about sin is to be the one who has sinned.

O Father, help me to understand that Your judgments are not retributive but remedial. You search me in order to save me. Amen.

'Life is decision'

FOR READING AND MEDITATION
COLOSSIANS 3:7–10

'But now you must rid yourselves of … anger, rage, malice, slander …' (v.8)

'Life,' said one philosopher, 'is *decision*.' We can decide to be angry or not be angry, to lie or not to lie, to use offensive language or not to use it. It is foolish to believe that these things just flow out of us of their own accord. Before angry or inappropriate words come from your mouth you have a moment of choice – to stop them or speak them. The moment of choice may be only a second – even a split second – but it is there nevertheless. If our lives are under the rule of Christ then it follows that our decisions will come under His rule as well. So it is just a question of willpower. You have to decide, 'I will no longer do this'. You supply the willingness – He will supply the power.

Father, I am going to strip off the filthy set of ill-fitting clothes and put them in the fire. Instead, I'm going to wear new clothes custom-made by Christ. Amen.

The charter of equality

FOR READING AND MEDITATION
COLOSSIANS 3:11

'Here there is no Greek or Jew ... but Christ is all, and is in all.' (v.11)

We live in an age seeking equality of opportunity for all, yet this verse, written so long ago, is *the* charter of equality. There just cannot be any distinctions in Christ. If you hold to distinctions then you cannot be in Christ. You are governed by something else. Then notice also the words 'Christ is all, and is in all'. What Paul means is this: Christ is all that matters. If Christ becomes all in all to us we cannot remain the people we were. What is more, everyone else becomes all in all also because we realise Christ dwells in them too. Why is the Church so slow in showing the world what a classless, raceless society is like? I am afraid there can only be one answer: Christ is not all in all.

O Father, You inspired Your servant Paul to sweep the decks of all discrimination. May we, Your people, fully implement it. Amen.

'Overalls or evening dress'

FOR READING AND MEDITATION
COLOSSIANS 3:12–14

'Therefore, as God's chosen people, holy and dearly loved, clothe yourselves with compassion ...' (v.12)

The reason God chose the people of Israel was that He wanted them to be His 'shop window' and reveal His love and holiness to other nations. Israel failed miserably in this respect, but it is Paul's hope and prayer that the church at Colosse – part of the new Israel of God – would treat others with the love God in Christ treated them. 'Love,' it has been said, 'is a colour that can be worn with anything – overalls or evening dress.' Or think of it as a kind of overcoat, if you like, a garment that covers all other virtues. It brings harmony to all disharmonies. Love is the garment the world sees. All other virtues are undergarments.

Father, help me to remember that virtues are of no value if love is not present, and that love makes all other virtues blend in unity. Amen.

Every church a haven?

FOR READING AND MEDITATION
COLOSSIANS 3:15

'Let the peace of Christ rule in your hearts ... And be thankful.' (v.15)

Paul is telling us here that when we are under the rule of Christ the inevitable result is that we experience peace in our relationships. Listen to the words of this verse again: '... since *as members of one body* you were called to peace'. Every Christian congregation can be a haven of peace. Isn't it a bit unrealistic, though, to expect Christians with different views, different backgrounds and different temperaments to live harmoniously with one another? Some might think so. But Paul wouldn't share that view. When Christ rules in the hearts of believers then peace will rule in that community of believers. Nothing could be more simple yet nothing, it seems, is more difficult.

Gracious Father, help us to see that for peace to rule we must come under Your rule. Amen.

Gratitude for grace

FOR READING AND MEDITATION
COLOSSIANS 3:16

'Let the word of Christ dwell in you richly as you teach and admonish one another …' (v.16)

What is being said here is this: the Word of God must control, not just us personally, but the whole Christian community, and all the ministries of the local church. It is to dwell in us fully as we teach, admonish, counsel, and so on. It is the Word of God, also, that must guide us as we sing. Some like to differentiate between psalms, hymns and spiritual songs, and they may well be right. However, what Paul has in mind here is not so much the different types of praise and worship, but the *content*. All the songs we sing in church should be consistent with the Word of God – that's his point. A gospel of good news must be echoed by songs of gratitude – gratitude for grace.

O God, You have saved us by grace; help us reflect that in the worship we offer to You. Amen.

'The Jesus Christ man'

FOR READING AND MEDITATION
COLOSSIANS 3:17

'And whatever you do, whether in word or deed, do it all in the name of the Lord Jesus ...' (v.17)

Dr E. Stanley Jones told of riding his bicycle in India and hearing a young boy who was a cowherd call out to another in the field, 'The Jesus Christ man is going along.' He said that when he heard those words he felt like getting off his bicycle and dropping to his knees in prayer that he might not do anything to destroy the village boys' estimation of him as a 'Jesus Christ man'. We are all to be Jesus Christ people – to do everything in His name. All that we do is to be done for Christ and in a Christlike manner. As a person once put it, 'We are the only Bible some people will read.' You are to do everything as representing Him, you are to do it in His name, in His stead, and in His Spirit.

Dear Father, I long to represent You today just as Christ represented You. Grant that my words and my actions may bring You glory. Amen.

A word to wives

FOR READING AND MEDITATION
COLOSSIANS 3:18

'Wives, submit to your husbands, as is fitting in the Lord.'
(v.18)

P aul now writes about family relationships. He has
a word for each member of the family: for wives it
is *submit*, for husbands it is *love and understand*, for
children it is *obey*. What does it mean for a Christian wife
to submit? Is it doing everything her husband demands
of her? I do not believe so. What if a husband asks his
wife to engage in something she is not comfortable with
because she knows it to be wrong? Is she to obey? Of
course not. Submission is a *disposition* – a disposition
to defer in everything that is right. It is not to be seen
as servility. A woman who practises biblical submission
will have a strong positive desire to support her husband
as he fulfils his role in the family.

O God, we live in a day when our culture contradicts the
teaching of Your Word. Help us to take Your way in the
clash between Christ and culture. Amen.

Love is ...

FOR READING AND MEDITATION
COLOSSIANS 3:19

'Husbands, love your wives and do not be harsh with them.' (v.19)

Paul is *commanding* love as if he knows that one of the easiest things in the world is for a husband to say to his wife, 'I love you', but then fail to demonstrate that love in practical ways. A woman told me, 'My husband's parting words to me when he goes off to work are, "I love you", but then I go to the bathroom, find his shaving kit lying around, the basin filthy, and towels strewn all over the floor. If he really loved me then he would clean up after him.' I agree. Love is not just something you say, love is something you do. Furthermore, if a tyrannical husband harshly says to his wife, 'The Word of God says you must submit', then in that action he has violated the law of love.

O God, strengthen my spirit as I follow a way of life that is governed by Your Word and not by the dictates of our culture. Amen.

How to serve the Lord

FOR READING AND MEDITATION
COLOSSIANS 3:20

'Children, obey your parents in everything, for this pleases the Lord.' (v.20)

On one occasion a family with a young son of 12 came to me. Although the boy had committed himself to Jesus Christ he was being somewhat rebellious towards his parents. He obviously loved the Lord, and as we talked about his Christian faith and what he wanted to do with his life, he told me that he would like to serve Christ in the field of Christian journalism. I asked him if he would be interested in knowing how he could express his desire to serve the Lord Jesus *at the present moment*. So I read him our text for today. Later his parents told me that the subsequent transformation in him was remarkable. He is now working for the Lord overseas, not as a journalist but as a preacher of the gospel.

Father, forgive us that we ask for guidance in running our families and yet sometimes balk at the directions You give us. Amen.

Problem fathers?

FOR READING AND MEDITATION
COLOSSIANS 3:21

'Fathers, do not embitter your children, or they will become discouraged.' (v.21)

Paul shows that not all the rights are on one side and all the duties on the other. Fathers, too, have a responsibility to their children. Coming down hard on children crushes their sensitive spirits. It is no good a father lamenting the fact that his child is not as strong and self-reliant as he himself is if he uses his strength to squash the child's fragile ego rather than develop it. Endless criticism, harsh punishments, unrealistic expectations, will have their effect in the long run. Many a child who is timid, fearful and plagued with deep feelings of inferiority and guilt has developed those characteristics not so much by nature as by nurture.

O Father, give our families another chance and help us to learn the ways of Your Word. In Jesus' name. Amen.

Free – on the inside

FOR READING AND MEDITATION
COLOSSIANS 3:22–24

'Slaves, obey your earthly masters in everything ... with sincerity of heart and reverence for the Lord.' (v.22)

Paul was writing, not to the leaders of society, but to the Church. Since he was unable to deal with the situation horizontally, he focuses on dealing with it vertically. He urges slaves to concentrate on the fact that they are working for the Lord and not for men. This change of perspective, Paul believed, would enable them to find inner freedom. Pagan slaves might obey out of fear of their master, but the Christian slave can obey for a different reason: to do it out of reverence for the Lord. And he reminded them of the reward they will receive – the divine inheritance. Paul was unable to give the slaves of his day the status of freedmen, but he certainly showed them how to be free on the inside.

Father, help me learn the lesson that even when I cannot change what is happening outside of me, I can change inwardly and find freedom in You. Amen.

A heated talking point

FOR READING AND MEDITATION
COLOSSIANS 3:25–4:1

'Masters, provide your slaves with what is right and fair, because … you also have a Master in heaven.' (4:1)

Once again (4:1) Paul presents the other side of an issue and, having addressed slaves, he has a word for their masters. Who was the greater wrongdoer, the slave who did not work as hard as he could or the master who was not considerate and did not give a proper reward? It must have been a new thought for slave masters that they should show consideration towards slaves, and I can imagine it becoming a heated talking point in the slave markets. Just as Christ showed fairness in the way He dealt with those who were slave masters so they, in turn, are to show fairness in the way they deal with their slaves. Both master and slave serve another Master – God in heaven.

Father, I see that to have mastery in life I must bow my knee to the Master. Your ways, and Your ways alone, are the ways of mastery. Amen.

First talk to God

FOR READING AND MEDITATION
COLOSSIANS 4:2–4

'Devote yourselves to prayer, being watchful and thankful.' (v.2)

Paul points out that before we talk to others about God we ought to talk to God about others. Evangelism is best undertaken in a spirit of prayer – by praying for people before talking to people. Sometimes I am astonished when I read training courses on evangelism and notice how little emphasis is placed on the need for personal, powerful intercessory prayer. Evangelistic techniques, methods, systems and procedures all have their place. However, they are of little value unless they have come from a heart that is given to prayer. Notice that when Paul talks about prayer he also adds this: 'being watchful and thankful'. Prayer needs to be coupled with praise, just as praise needs to be coupled with prayer.

Father, drive this truth deep within my spirit – that before I talk to people about You, I must talk to You about people. In Jesus' name. Amen.

The right to say 'No'

FOR READING AND MEDITATION
COLOSSIANS 4:5–6

'Be wise in the way you act towards outsiders …' (v.5)

P aul is thinking not only about *what* we say but *how* we say it. Many are not wise in the way they share their faith. They are insensitive and intrusive. A dear old Christian wrote in the flyleaf of my Bible: 'To win some be winsome.' Evangelism should never be a 'hard sell'. We take advantage of every opportunity to share Christ, even offer Him, but we must always respect the right of the person to whom we are witnessing to say 'No'. There was an occasion when Jesus talked to a rich ruler, who could not accept what Jesus told him and turned away (Luke 18:18–25). Did Jesus run after him, and try to press him into making a decision? No, He let him go because He respected his right to say 'No'.

Father, forgive me if I put people off by insensitivity and aggressiveness. May I present the gospel clearly and in a gracious manner. Amen.

Paul – a people-person

FOR READING AND MEDITATION
COLOSSIANS 4:7–9

'Tychicus ... a dear brother, a faithful minister and fellow-servant in the Lord.' (v.7)

Paul was a true people-person. He did not just remember names; he cared deeply for those whom he counted as his friends. Paul was greatly loved because he loved greatly. This part of his letter is rich in personal messages and greetings. Some Christian workers are faithful servants but not very 'dear', and not good 'fellow-servants' either. This is particularly true of the strong, devoted, driven types. They are extremely busy and absorbed in fulfilling their mission, but no one would ever refer to them as 'dear'. And they are so taken up with their own ministry that they cannot work with others. Tychicus was a well-rounded person, faithful in his ministry, a dear brother and a fellow-worker.

Father, I too would be a well-rounded person. Help me submerge my will and affection in a larger Will and Affection. Amen.

More names on the list

FOR READING AND MEDITATION
COLOSSIANS 4:10–13

'Epaphras … is always wrestling in prayer for you …' (v.12)

The phrase 'wrestling in prayer' suggests that the prayers of Epaphras were largely intercessory. What an insight Paul must have gained into the character of Epaphras during their time together in Rome as he listened to him pray for the church back at Colosse. The foundations of this man's character were set deep in the soil of prayer. There is no doubt in my mind that the secret of Epaphras's spiritual success lay in his prayer life. He was great in soul because he prayed much, and because he prayed with the unselfishness which marked all he did. Earnest and persistent prayer was the secret of his sanctity. That secret is available to us all.

Father, forgive me if I do not commune regularly with You and intercede for others in prayer. Help me to see prayer as not just a luxury, but a necessity. Amen.

Final greetings

FOR READING AND MEDITATION
COLOSSIANS 4:14–16

'After this letter has been read to you, see that it is also read in the church of the Laodiceans ...' (v.16)

Paul turns from sending specific greetings to giving more general greetings – to the brothers at Laodicea, and to Nympha and the church in her house. Generally the Early Church met for worship, instruction and fellowship in homes, as we can see from such verses as Romans 16:5, 1 Corinthians 16:19, Philemon 2 and Acts 12:12. Paul asks that his letter be read in the Laodicean church as well, and the Colossians in turn were to read the letter from Laodicea. Obviously Paul also wanted the Laodicean believers to be aware of possible threats to their faith. This exchange of letters shows the importance of reading all we can. The more Scripture we absorb the stronger our defences against false teaching will be.

Father, may I be diligent in my reading of Scripture. Help me learn all I can so that I may not waver in my faith. Amen.

Say 'No' to the marginal

FOR READING AND MEDITATION
COLOSSIANS 4:17

'Tell Archippus: "See to it that you complete the work you have received in the Lord."' (v.17)

There is a slight suggestion in these words that Archippus was a man who did not find it easy to follow through on things. The temptation to do the easier things and not to follow through on issues plagues us all. Paul's words – 'See to it that you complete the work you have received in the Lord' – strike home to every one of us I am sure. Notice the words *you have received in the Lord*. Everybody *in the Lord* is in service for the Lord. It means being involved in the Lord's plans for us. Let no unimportant weeds choke the fine wheat of the kingdom of God. Say 'No' to the marginal so that you can say 'Yes' to the central. And do not give up, but complete the work God has given you to do.

Lord Jesus Christ, You fulfilled Your Father's purposes in everything that You had to do. Help me, too, fulfil the ministry You have chosen for me. Amen.

Closing words

FOR READING AND MEDITATION
COLOSSIANS 4:18

'I, Paul, write this greeting in my own hand. Remember my chains. Grace be with you.' (v.18)

We come now to Paul's last words to the church at Colosse: 'Remember my chains. Grace be with you'. One of the greatest evidences of spiritual maturity is the desire, when under personal pressure or pain, to still reach out and give to others. Paul was such a man. In the midst of overwhelming difficulties his final thought is for others. So ends an important letter, one written with the desire to prevent believers being drawn away from the truth of the gospel, and one in which Paul has encouraged us to see Christ as all-sufficient and all-supreme. Christ is 'all, and is in all' (3:11). Let me put my last thought in the form of this highly personal question: We are all in all to Christ, but *is Christ all in all to us?*

O Father, I offer myself to You again today and pray that just as Your Son is the centre of Your universe so may He be the centre of my universe. Amen.

Danger! Fire!

FOR READING AND MEDITATION
LUKE 12:49–59

'I have come to bring fire on the earth, and how I wish it were already kindled!' (v.49)

Two kinds of fire are burning in this universe – one destructive, the other divine. These blazing flames – the one from heaven and the other from hell – compete for our attention; both seek to engulf us, both seek to ignite and motivate us. And the truth is this: the fire to which we get closer, the one we allow to consume us, is the one that will determine our spiritual destiny – both here and hereafter. Jesus speaks of His heavenly fire but James warns: 'The tongue also is a fire, a world of evil among the parts of the body. It corrupts the whole person, sets the whole course of his life on fire, and is itself set on fire by hell' (James 3:6). What kind of fire has got hold of you?

Father, help me not to hesitate – I want to be consumed by Your fire. Help me to come closer than ever before to the heavenly flame. Amen.

A framework of fire

FOR READING AND MEDITATION
HEBREWS 12:25–29; MATTHEW 25:34–41

'... for our "God is a consuming fire."' (Heb. 12:29)
'Depart ... into the eternal fire ...' (Matt. 25:41)

Ian Macpherson points out that here on this earth we live between two great natural fires: a fire above us in the heart of the sun, and a fire beneath us in the heart of the earth. My spiritual illustration is: the fire from above is creative, vitalising, beneficent; the fire from beneath is convulsive, frightening, catastrophic. One maintains life; the other expresses itself in the awful destructiveness of a volcano. The fire that comes from heaven is purifying, vivifying and beautifying; the fires of hell are threatening, intimidating and destructive. Which fire will we choose to turn to? Which fire will we give ourselves to? I have made my choice – it is the fire from heaven. How about you?

Father, help me choose to turn my whole being in the direction of Your creative life giving fire from heaven. In Jesus' name I pray. Amen.

'Redeemed from fire by fire'

FOR READING AND MEDITATION
MALACHI 3:1–12

'For he will be like a refiner's fire ...' (v.2)

T.S. Eliot wrote: 'To be redeemed from fire by fire ...'
What does Eliot mean? He is thinking of the fact
that some fires can be overwhelmed only by a stronger,
fiercer flame. Consider some of the fires that burn today
– fires of moral permissiveness, fires of extremist Islamic
militancy and fires of terrorism. Those who fan the flames
of these fires have a passion – a passion to spread their
message to the whole world. Make no mistake about it,
there is a fire burning in their hearts. And the only way
such fire can be overwhelmed is by the fire of the Holy
Spirit, burning and blazing in the hearts of people who
have had an encounter with the fire-baptising Christ.

*Father, grant that the flame of Your Spirit may burn in my
heart with such fierce heat and intensity that it will quench
all other fires. Amen.*

'The only hope ...'

FOR READING AND MEDITATION
HEBREWS 1:1–7

'He makes ... his servants flames of fire.' (v.7)

Many years ago, as I left the city of Belfast after a number of buildings were set on fire during the troubles, a friend of mine shook my hand and said, 'In Northern Ireland it's going to be a race between Christianity and political ideology, *but a flame of fire will win*.' Despite the difficulties of the past, Christians in Northern Ireland show evidence of being more on fire for God today than they have ever been. The only way hatred is ever truly quelled is by being engulfed in the fire of God's love, which burns in the hearts of those who are redeemed. The only hope for this mixed-up, confused and angry generation is to be redeemed from fire – by fire.

O Father, may we be consumed by the Holy Spirit's fire. Let Your fire burn in me – this day and every day. Amen.

'This rabble of the passions'

FOR READING AND MEDITATION
GALATIANS 5:16–26

*'The acts of the sinful nature are obvious: sexual
immorality, impurity and debauchery …' (v.19)*

The ravaging fire of unrestrained moral permissiveness
has been dubbed, 'This rabble of the passions'. The
fires intended for the furnace to run the ship are in danger
of destroying it. In his youth, the mystical English poet,
John Donne, sported the family crest which consisted
of a sheaf of snakes. One writer says of this, 'It was
an appropriate symbol of the vipers of passion which,
unholy and unruly, nested in his bosom.' The day came,
however, when John Donne met Jesus Christ, and the fire
of unbridled passion that burned in him was engulfed by
the heavenly flame – so much so that he changed the
family crest with its coiled serpents to one in which was
depicted the form of the crucified Saviour.

*Father, I see that the only way to be released from 'this
rabble of the passions' is to be engulfed with a stronger and
purer passion – Your passion. Amen.*

Reprobate instincts

FOR READING AND MEDITATION
ROMANS 1:18–32

'Therefore God gave them over in the sinful desires of their hearts to sexual impurity ...' (v.24)

When our natural appetite for sex is expressed in accordance with God's guidelines, it is a wonderful gift. Sadly, for some it is a burning passion that is out of control and quietly, yet surely, destroys their lives. When translating Romans 1:28 Moffatt used the phrase 'reprobate instinct' – it is an instinct naturally right but turned reprobate. Millions, around the world are being engulfed in the devastating flames of HIV/AIDS, because, as Paul says, 'they did not think it worthwhile to retain the knowledge of God' (v.28). Sex is a fire. Within the moral guidelines set down by God, passionate sex is wonderful; treated unwisely, as happens so frequently in today's world, it will burn.

O Father, help men and women to understand that Your moral guidelines are not given to repress us but to release us. Amen.

'The song of all songs'

FOR READING AND MEDITATION
ECCLESIASTES 12:8–14

'Fear God and keep his commandments, for this is the whole duty of man.' (v.13)

L isten carefully to what Solomon is saying: 'The song of all songs …' 'Oh for a kiss from your lips!' The chief emphasis is sex. Other life philosophies could be stated in the same way: 'The song of all songs – Oh for a large bank account!' What is the chief emphasis in life … sex, money, fame? Yet Solomon said, 'when I surveyed all that my hands had done … everything was meaningless …' (Eccl. 2:10–11). Why was his life so meaningless? It was because he was seeking the wrong things first. No age has emphasised sex more than this age, and yet no age has enjoyed it less. Restraints have been abandoned and the world, generally speaking, has gone in for 'thrills', only to find that in the thrills are ills.

Father, baptise me with heavenly fire that my 'song of all songs' be of You. In Jesus' name I pray. Amen.

The worst thing about anger ...

FOR READING AND MEDITATION
ESTHER 1:1–12

'Then the king became furious and burned with anger.'
(v.12)

Another fateful flame is the fire of uncontrolled hatred and anger. Every day millions are being consumed by the flames of hatred and anger, and yet they do not realise it. We say, 'He burns me up'. It's true; he does. We used to think that getting mad at someone took its toll only on the person we got mad at, but now, in the cold light of science, the fallacy of that belief is being revealed. The worst thing about anger is being the person who holds the anger. Doctors are more aware than ever of the long-term effects of anger on our physical bodies, particularly stress and blood pressure. Hatred and anger are fatal fires that, if not quenched by the fire of God's love, can kill – literally.

O God, I see that I pass on to my body the health or sickness of my spirit and my soul. I long to be healthy in spirit, soul and body. Amen.

Anger is poison

FOR READING AND MEDITATION
ECCLESIASTES 7:1–12

*'Do not be quickly provoked in your spirit, for anger
resides in the lap of fools.' (v.9)*

Three emotions – irritation, indignation and resentment – can reverberate within us without being expressed. They arise when the mind continues to focus on the cause of an offence and will not allow it to pass. The feelings are then kept simmering, day after day, week after week. Hatred and anger, however, are different; they are strong emotions that soon reveal themselves. When irritated or resentful, we may clam up; when angry or hating, we usually blow up. If they are allowed to increase, hatred and anger develop into rage and fury. None of these emotions are things to joke about – they must be recognised, understood and dealt with. Believe me, if you don't control them, they will control you.

*O God my Father, I realise that if I live with my resentments
I will not be able to live with myself. Help me deal with
these emotions. Amen.*

Being angry – yet without sin

FOR READING & MEDITATION
MARK 3:1–6

'He looked round at them in anger and, deeply distressed at their stubborn hearts, said to the man, "Stretch out your hand."' (v.5)

Ephesians 4:26 in the Authorised Version says: 'Be ye angry, and sin not.' Some say it's OK to be angry and vent powerful emotions of anger but notice those vital words *'and sin not'*. How is it possible for us to be angry without committing sin? The answer is by being angry at nothing but sin. In the passage we have read today we see our Lord demonstrating a fierce but righteous anger. Anger is righteous when it is grief at sin and we are not holding a grudge. If we are honest, though, most of our anger is occasioned by self-concern – and thus is unrighteous. Jesus was angry – and did not sin. In Him the fire of anger was under control— and how!

O Father, I see that hatred and anger can eat like acid into my moral nature. Purify me with Your holy fire. In Jesus' name I pray. Amen.

Pentecost – a prophecy fulfilled

FOR READING AND MEDITATION
MATTHEW 3:1–12

'I baptise you with water ... He will baptise you with the Holy Spirit and with fire.' (v.11)

Were John's words just a figure of speech – a picturesque way of describing a spiritual experience? In the upper room a new power pulses through the disciples, causing them to speak in languages they have never learned and they are instantly transformed. They watch as tongues of fire appear on each other's heads (Acts 2:1–13). At once all their hesitancy and trepidation is consumed and they pour out on to the crowded streets of Jerusalem to spread the wonderful news that Jesus is alive. What has happened to their fear? It has been swallowed up in the fire of the Holy Spirit. From that moment they are like men and women who are ablaze; they have indeed been baptised with the Holy Spirit – and with fire!

Father, I cannot be content with a flickering spiritual experience; I long for one that is engulfed in flame. Set me alight, set me on fire. Amen.

The flame of jealousy

FOR READING AND MEDITATION
PROVERBS 6:27–35

'… for jealousy arouses a husband's fury, and he will show no mercy when he takes revenge.' (v.34)

Another fire that ravages is the fire of ungodly jealousy. It is destructive, malicious and poisonous. I have seen an entire community disrupted by jealousy. It happened in a small town in Yorkshire, where a manager of a mill was so jealous of another man that he brought about the complete closure of the place, putting hundreds of people out of work. A whole community was devastated – just to satisfy one person's jealousy. Satisfy? Hardly. Within a year the jealous man became crippled with arthritis and within two years he was dead. The newspapers reported, 'He died a bitter man.' Make no mistake – out of all the fires that consume, jealousy is the one with the fiercest flames.

O Father, give me the grace and power to deal – and deal effectively – with the ravaging flames of jealousy. In Christ's name I pray. Amen.

How jealousy works ...

FOR READING AND MEDITATION
ROMANS 12:9–21

'Honour one another above yourselves.' (v.10)

W hat exactly is jealousy? It is the pain or displeasure we sometimes feel at the happiness, success, or the imagined superiority of another. It is the hurt we feel when someone with whom we match ourselves surpasses us. It is also that secret elation we feel when someone we dislike stumbles and falls. Jealousy is deadly in its nature and it never fails to scar and scorch the soul. Jealousy works, not by leaping a chasm, but by getting into the crevices. We are rarely jealous of the people we do not know; jealousy is focused on those closest to us. It is not normally directed against those who completely eclipse us, but those who *just* outdo us – who compete in the same circle for the esteem we covet.

Father, I ask myself: How do I feel when I hear my friends praised? If You see in me the tiniest ripple of jealousy, root it out, I pray. Amen.

John-ward or Jesus-ward?

FOR READING AND MEDITATION
JOHN 21:15–23

'Peter turned and saw … the disciple whom Jesus loved … he asked, "Lord, what about him?"' (vv.20–21)

John the Baptist's disciples came to him and said, 'Rabbi, that man who was with you on the other side of the Jordan – the one you testified about – well, he is baptising, and everyone is going to him.' John replied that he was full of joy to serve the bridegroom and hear His voice (John 3:26,29). In other words, 'I know my place. I'm secure in my calling and am content with it.' Contrast today's reading where Peter seems to have been afflicted by jealousy: 'When Peter saw [John], he asked, "Lord, what about him?"' Imagine it – Peter had just had a wonderful encounter with Christ, but there was still a little lingering jealousy. He looked John-ward instead of Jesus-ward.

Father, help me to rejoice in the joy of all Your children. May I take pleasure in their successes and all their honours. Amen.

The desire to possess

FOR READING AND MEDITATION
1 TIMOTHY 6:1–10

'For the love of money is a root of all kinds of evil ...' (v.10)

Another fierce flame is the fire of acquisitiveness – the all-consuming desire to possess money and material things. For many people their chief goal in life is to get their hands on things. They burn with desire to have more and more and more. We cannot despise money or material things for without them life on this earth would be difficult. But for many, material things become such a priority that they push out everything else. People become covetous, grasping and greedy. The inability of things to satisfy the deep craving for life and meaning has been demonstrated in every age. And yet people still pursue money and material possessions with a passion that should be reserved for God alone.

O Father, grant that the fire of acquisitiveness shall not burn in my heart. And please deliver me from all false values and false goals. Amen.

Money, money, money

FOR READING AND MEDITATION
LUKE 16:1–15

'... You cannot serve both God and Money.' (v.13)

People who regard money and material things as evils in themselves have a wrong perspective on the issue. Money itself is not evil. It enables the hungry to be fed, the homeless to be given shelter, and medical treatment to be provided for those who are sick. No, it is not money that is the dangerous thing – it is the excessive *love* of it that consumes and the soul becomes as metallic as the coinage that is accumulated. Friendship, family, appreciation of life and spiritual sensitivity may each be sacrificed to this one absorbing passion. When the winter of materialism sets in, it is a very frosty season. May our passion not be in our possessions, but let *God's* possession be our passion.

Father, help me see that You have made us in Your image and that we cannot live successfully if we try to live in the image of the material. Amen.

Never enough!

FOR READING AND MEDITATION
ECCLESIASTES 5:10–20

'Whoever loves money never has money enough; whoever loves wealth is never satisfied with his income ...' (v.10)

I say once more that the danger of wealth does not lie in *possessing* a large amount of money; it is the inordinate *longing* to be rich that is the deadly thing. A person is consumed with the flames of acquisitiveness when he or she puts too high a value on money, and loves and longs for nothing else. Some are so affected by it that they evaluate other men and women simply in terms of how much or how little they possess. Anything that weakens the conviction that our security lies solely in God is dangerous – and nothing weakens that conviction more than the love of money. Our text says, 'Whoever loves money never has money enough.' Why? It is because that person doesn't have the money – the money has them.

O God, please help me for I live in an acquisitive society where worth tends to be judged by wealth. May my decisions be Christlike ones. Amen.

'Unpurchasable people'

FOR READING AND MEDITATION
LUKE 12:13–21

'Be on your guard against all kinds of greed; a man's life does not consist in the abundance of his possessions.' (v.15)

Professor W.E. Hocking has argued that we cannot have a sound society unless we have a sufficient number of men and women who cannot be bought. He has termed them 'unpurchasable people'. And Jesus Christ specialises in producing such 'unpurchasable people'. This is not to say there are no 'unpurchasable people' outside the Church, for clearly there are. It is just that Jesus Christ produces far more of them because He transforms them from within and reminds them of the need to be 'rich towards God' (v.21). The people who have caught the spirit of Jesus, and whose lives have been set on fire by Him, are emancipated from slavery to things. They enjoy them, but they are not ruled by them.

O God, again I pray that You will preserve me from the cravings and desires that can so easily be fanned into a blaze. Amen.

How few look really happy

FOR READING AND MEDITATION
2 TIMOTHY 3:1–9

'There will be terrible times in the last days. People will be ... lovers of pleasure rather than lovers of God ...'
(vv. 1–4)

Another fire that can burn with an all-consuming passion is hedonism – the love and pursuit of pleasure. Freud was right about one thing when he said that pleasure is a chief hunger in the human heart, and that we will never understand why people behave the way they do unless we see their behaviour in terms of a desire to have that hunger met. All across the world we see the smoke and flame of this false fire burning with a fierce intensity. Yet few look really happy – especially the day after a night of excess in pubs, clubs or casinos! How sad that so many are looking everywhere for peace and joy – everywhere except the one place where it can be found.

O God, how I thank You that my search for life ended when I found You. Blessed be Your glorious and wondrous name. Amen.

Nothing!

FOR READING AND MEDITATION
LUKE 23:1–12

'He plied him with many questions, but Jesus gave him no answer.' (v.9)

King Herod was a hedonist. The historian Josephus tells us that he was known all over the Roman empire for his love of pleasure, and he enjoyed nothing more than bringing a new form of entertainment to his palace. Herod looked to Jesus for entertainment and pleasure: 'he hoped to see him perform some miracle' (v.8). We read that Herod plied Jesus with many questions 'but Jesus gave him no answer'. Christ had answered the question Pilate put to Him – so why did He not respond to Herod? Why did He say nothing? I think it was because Jesus refused to entertain those who were self-seeking, who did not take Him seriously. When pleasure takes precedence over truth then the lips of our Lord are silent.

Lord Jesus Christ, Son of God and Saviour of my soul, may I take seriously everything You say and everything You do. Amen.

'A new dark age'

FOR READING AND MEDITATION
TITUS 3:1–5

'At one time we too were foolish, disobedient, deceived and enslaved by all kinds of passions and pleasures.'
(v.3)

Charles Colson, once adviser to President Nixon and now a transformed Christian, says in *Against the Night* that we are in the midst of a new dark age – a fiercely hedonistic culture. He makes the point that when men and women lose the sense of God they are then drawn to pleasure and entertainment as a means of filling up the vacuum in their souls. Newspapers are filled with features and adverts for entertainment – yet at one time Spurgeon's sermons made the front page! In this age, God is fading from people's minds and, like thoughtless children, they believe that the toy-land of pleasure will soothe their restlessness. But though the fires of hedonism may burn, unlike the divine fire, they are destined to burn out.

O God, when I see this happening around me I feel like crying out: 'Turn to Christ'. Use me, dear Lord, to show someone who is lost the way to You. Amen.

'Animated bubbles'

FOR READING AND MEDITATION
TITUS 3:5–11

'These things are excellent and profitable for everyone.'
(v.8)

I f we do away with God then we have no framework of
reference, no star by which to steer the ship of our life,
and so we are tossed from wave to wave of futile pursuits
– we have no star and no harbour. If there is no God to
give worth and meaning to life then, as someone has put
it, 'We are only animated bubbles that rise to the cosmic
surface, glisten in the sunlight for a brief space and then
burst, leaving a nasty wet spot on the surface of things.'
Or, to change the figure, 'Life is a fretful child that must
be played with until it falls to sleep.' Without God we go
through an endless succession of meaningless days.

O God, all around us we see the destructive flames of the
devil. Burn in me, dear Lord – to the glory and honour of
Your precious name. Amen.

The Way and not-the-way

FOR READING AND MEDITATION
NUMBERS 32:14–23

'… be sure that your sin will find you out.' (v.23)

Kant said, 'Two things strike me with awe: the starry heavens above and the moral law within'. The God who established the laws that guide the spinning planets is the God who laid down the moral laws that guide and govern our lives on this earth. It is clear, as Dr. E. Stanley Jones pointed out, that there are two roads through life: the Way, and not-the-way. Pilots must obey the way of the laws on which flying depends – or else! When our lawmakers, in their zeal to experience freedom, reject the moral laws that God has established in the universe, they go down a way that is not-the-way. When we violate God's moral law the effects register in us; we get the consequences and our lives crash in pieces.

Father, may our lawmakers and politicians understand that You are the Creator of both worlds – the world above and the world within. Amen.

What history teaches us ...

FOR READING AND MEDITATION
JUDGES 17:1–13

'In those days Israel had no king; everyone did as he saw fit.' (v.6)

I n his great work, *A Study of History*, Arnold Toynbee argues that the characteristic of a civilisation that is on the way out is a widespread contempt for moral law and order. If that is the case then, as far as Britain is concerned, I say – God help us. Those in the media are presenting an image of life that conveys this: do exactly as you please as long as it does not offend the person you are doing it with. No mention, you notice, of whether or not it is an offence to God. The sparks of one generation become the fires of the next. And we who know Christ must realise, also, that there is only one fire that can engulf the fires of moral laxity and permissiveness; it is the fire of God.

O Father, send the burning, blazing fire of the Holy Spirit upon us to engulf all other fires. Send us another Pentecost, we plead. Amen.

Wild fanaticism

FOR READING AND MEDITATION
ACTS 7:54–8:3

'And Saul was there, giving approval to his death.' (8:1)

There is a consuming passion that inflames the hearts of those who are caught in the grip of a fierce fanaticism. Saul of Tarsus was a fanatic before he met Christ. But when he did, his wild nature was transformed and he changed from being a fanatic to an ardent follower. The first modern example of wild fanaticism that comes to mind is that of Nazism. Many people still alive saw this devastating fire consume a whole nation and leave it in ashes. I can also remember listening to a man, who is now a committed follower of Christ, describe how his fanaticism led him to plant bombs that maimed and killed people. Such is the power of fanaticism – a devastating, destructive fire that scars and blinds the soul.

Oh God, thank You that You laid Your hand on a fanatic like Saul and turned him into one of the greatest disciples the world has ever seen. Amen.

'Stalin' or the Saviour?

FOR READING AND MEDITATION
ACTS 4:1–12

'Salvation is found in no-one else, for there is no other name under heaven … by which we must be saved.' (v.12)

Fanatical ideologies, whether political, racial or religious, are often fed by the oppression and grievances of subject peoples, and also by a thirst and lust for power. What makes a philosophy dangerous is not its ideology, but the fanatical fire that burns in the hearts of its advocates. The Russian composer Prokofiev rhapsodises about Stalin: *'Stalin'* – *I say to the universe; 'Stalin'* – *and I add nothing.* Stalin's name was made to include all things – the party, the country, everything. That's fire – dangerous fire. Will the fire that burns in the hearts of Christ's followers win over the fire that burns in the hearts of other world systems and ideologies? We wait and see.

O God, we are passing through a turbulent time in history. Help me to see that I belong to Your kingdom 'for such a time as this'. Amen.

The answer to fire – is fire

FOR READING AND MEDITATION
1 CHRONICLES 21:18–30

*'He called on the Lord, and the Lord answered him with
fire from heaven on the altar of burnt offering.' (v.26)*

It must be emphasised, of course, that everyone
is free to commit himself or herself to a cause. But
when people allow themselves to be overtaken by a
fiery fanaticism that leads them to act in ways that
violate moral and civil law, then their actions must be
denounced and repudiated. All the major religions of
the world have had their share of fanatics who, by their
burning passion, are driven to extreme acts of violence.
That fire within them is a terrible, destructive fire. What
is the answer to all of these different destructive fires?
How can these fires which roar out of hell be engulfed
and brought under control? The answer is Pentecost and
the fire of God that comes down from heaven.

*O God, prepare my heart to receive all that You have for
me. Father, I long to be more on fire. Hear my prayer, in
Christ's name. Amen.*

The 'rabble' – redeemed

FOR READING AND MEDITATION
JOHN 6:60–71

'The Spirit gives life; the flesh counts for nothing.' (v.63)

One of the most thrilling things about Pentecost is that it introduces us, not to a fire that ravages, but to a fire that redeems. The fire that comes from above overwhelms the fire that comes from below. Remember how John Donne's lustful life was transformed? It was not a scolding from his parents; it was not resolutions and subduing the will; it was the incoming of Christ's love in the power of the Holy Spirit. When a new fire began to burn on the altar of his soul – he was redeemed from fire by fire.

Am I talking to someone now whose life is controlled by turbulent passions – maybe the lure of internet pornography? Open your whole being to the flame of God. You, too, can be redeemed from fire – by fire.

O God, let Your holy fire consume all the dross and the evil desires that may have a grip on my life. In Jesus' name I ask it. Amen.

The open road

FOR READING AND MEDITATION
2 CORINTHIANS 5:11-21

'For Christ's love compels us, because we are convinced that one died for all, and therefore all died.' (v.14)

In my early years I used to give all sorts of practical advice to those troubled by their sexual desires. I have come to see that although my ideas made a lot of sense, in reality they were only the fences along an open road. That open road is the experience of the passion and love of Jesus Christ moving in one's soul. We can expel a desire only by a higher and stronger desire. The fire of God's love burning in our hearts is the only fire that can engulf and extinguish all other fires. None of the boundaries we build in our lives can save us unless the fire of God is at work within us. When your heart is ablaze with the love of Christ then you are free. 'Love Christ and do what you like,' said Augustine. For in loving Christ you will do what is right.

Lord Jesus Christ, let the fire of Your love fall upon my lesser loves so that all my loves may be lost in You. Amen.

Don't fight – surrender

FOR READING AND MEDITATION
MATTHEW 13:24–30

'... *collect the weeds and tie them in bundles to be burned ...*' (*v.30*)

There are times in the Christian life when we must 'fight the good fight of the faith' (1 Tim. 6:12), but there are times when fighting is not appropriate. We are to fight for truth and Christian doctrine, we are to fight for Christian standards in society, we are to fight against evil powers and authorities, but when it comes to dealing with 'the rabble of the passions', the operative word is not 'fight' but 'surrender'. To fight the passions involves focusing attention on them. And it is a well-known law of the personality that whatever gets your attention gets you. When you no longer fight your passions but surrender them to God then your attention is drawn from them to Him.

Father, Your burning is what I need. Burn out of me, I pray, everything that is not of You. In Jesus' name I ask it. Amen.

There's more!

FOR READING AND MEDITATION
ACTS 1:12–26

' ... *Peter stood up among the believers (a group numbering about a hundred and twenty) ...*' (v.15)

W hy were there just 120 present in the upper room? In 1 Corinthians 15:6 we read that after the resurrection Jesus appeared to 'more than five hundred'. What happened to the others – a group of at least 380? They had witnessed the risen Christ but wonderful though this is – there's more. God offers to all those who know His Son not only the joy of regeneration but the thrill of a mighty baptism in the Spirit. To have seen the triumphant Jesus on the other side of the tomb must have been an amazing and thrilling experience. Any one of the disciples could be forgiven for thinking that there was nothing more marvellous than that. The truth was, however, that this was not so. There was more.

O Father, may I not be content with receiving only Your lesser blessings. I long for everything You have to give me. Everything! Amen.

Do we get all at conversion?

FOR READING AND MEDITATION
ACTS 11:1–18

'Then I remembered what the Lord had said: "John baptised with water, but you will be baptised with the Holy Spirit."' (v.16)

A s soon as I make the claim that there's more for a Christian to experience than an initial encounter with the risen Lord Jesus, there will be those who say, 'I received all of the Spirit it is possible to have when I came to know the Lord at my conversion.' The attitude I have adopted towards those who disagree with me on the point that the baptism of the Spirit is additional to, and different from, conversion is to say, 'If you want to believe that you had everything at your conversion then the question I would put to you is this: What is your spiritual experience like now? Can you say at this moment that your life is on fire for God? And if not, why not?' Lovingly, I say it again – there's more.

O God, help me to evaluate my life, not only in the light of the past, but also in the light of the present. Please give me more of Your Spirit – now. Amen.

A life change – life-changing

FOR READING AND MEDITATION
ACTS 9:1–19

'"Who are you, Lord?" Saul asked. "I am Jesus, whom you are persecuting," he replied.' (v.5)

There is something more for Saul than an encounter with the risen Christ, great and wonderful though that is – there is a mighty baptism in the Holy Spirit through Ananias (v.17). Saul's life was changed but more than that – he became life-changing. In verses 23 to 25 we read, 'After many days had gone by, the Jews conspired to kill him … But his followers took him by night and lowered him in a basket through an opening in the wall.' Look again at the words 'many days … his followers'. In a mere matter of 'many days' after his conversion and filling with the Spirit he had gained many followers. This is true spiritual fruitfulness! He was not only on fire for God – he set other hearts on fire also!

Father, set my heart on fire with Your Spirit and with Your love so that I may kindle the same fire in others. Amen.

Fire! Fire! Fire!

FOR READING AND MEDITATION
ACTS 2:29–39

'The promise is for you and your children ... for all whom the Lord our God will call.' (v.39)

Perhaps there is no more striking experience of being filled with the Spirit than that of Blaise Pascal. This exceptional inventor and genius, who died when he was only 39, wrote the brilliant satire – *The Letters of a Provincial* – and his *Pensées* is one of the most powerful books on Christian thought that has ever been written. He came to know Christ when he was 25, but it was not until six years later that he received a baptism in the Holy Spirit. The record of this experience was found sewn into his waistcoat after his death. This is what it said: 'The year of grace 1654, Monday, November 23. From about half-past ten at night to about half-past twelve. Fire! Fire! Fire!'

O God, my heart is open. Come, Holy Spirit, come. Set my whole being alight with Your holy fire. In Jesus' name I pray. Amen.

'A stone in the heart'

FOR READING AND MEDITATION
EZEKIEL 11:16–25

'I will … put a new spirit in them; I will remove from them their heart of stone and give them a heart of flesh.' (v.19)

Can the fire of God redeem us from hatred and anger? A woman of 70 admitted, 'I have lived most of my life with a stone in my heart. It has been there ever since the day my mother said to me, "I hate you", because I stood in the way of her going to another man.' I sat with this woman as she surrendered her deeply repressed anger to Christ. As I did so I saw the divine fire at work in her as within minutes the stone in her heart had gone. A sick missionary with inner anger said, 'Suddenly the Holy Spirit fell upon me. I felt Him burn up the anger that was deep within me. Afterwards I got up and have not had a day's sickness since. Now my doctor says laughingly that I'm so healthy I'm ready for hard labour.'

O God, burn in me until all sinful hatred and anger are burned out of me. In Christ's name I pray. Amen.

'The first word in Christianity'

FOR READING AND MEDITATION
ROMANS 7:14–25

*'Who will rescue me from this body of death? Thanks be
to God – through Jesus Christ our Lord!' (vv.24–25)*

Christian books are full of helpful advice on how to
deal with sinful hatred and anger. But we must be
willing to trust the Holy Spirit with our whole being,
and allow Him to burn out any impurities there are in
us. And here's my point: unless we are willing to get
close enough to Christ for Him to immerse us in the
flame of the Spirit then the Christian life becomes just an
exercise of the will – try harder. Sadly, many are caught
up in the 'try harder' syndrome. They do not realise that
the first word in Christianity is trust, and the second is
try. Get those words the wrong way round and you are
in trouble. The more you understand what it means to
trust, the easier it will be to obey.

*O God save me from getting these words – trust and try
– the wrong way round, for I see it is a vitally important
matter. In Jesus' name. Amen.*

The refining fire

FOR READING AND MEDITATION
JEREMIAH 23:25–32

'"Is not my word like fire," declares the Lord ...' (v.29)

Behind most hatred and anger is a touchy, unsurrendered self. When the will is surrendered to Christ and the Holy Spirit, and a divine fire is allowed to burn within, then there is nothing in us waiting to be triggered off by circumstances or what others say about us. Suspect a self that can explode in hatred and anger – it is probably diseased with self-centredness. Difficult though this may be to believe, it is often easier to 'try harder' than to trust Christ and to believe that the Holy Spirit will come with His searching, scorching fire into the secret places of the soul. But with Charles Wesley we say: *Refining fire, go through my heart ... And sanctify the whole.*

O Father, show me the foolishness of depending on myself, and help me to put trusting ahead of trying. In Jesus' name I pray. Amen.

'I pray for him daily'

FOR READING AND MEDITATION
DEUTERONOMY 4:15–24

'For the Lord your God is a consuming fire …' (v.24)

Can God's heavenly fire overcome the hellish fire of jealousy? When the famous preacher Dr Meyer saw that Dr Campbell Morgan attracted larger crowds, he confessed to more than one person that he found himself liable to bouts of jealousy. One day, realising that he could not continue like this any longer, he fell on his knees, surrendered himself afresh to Christ, and asked that the fire of the Holy Spirit might overwhelm the flames of jealousy that had began to sear his soul. When, later, a close friend asked him whether he had been able to deal with his jealousy in connection with Dr Campbell Morgan, he replied, 'Oh yes, God has greatly helped me in this; now I pray for him daily.'

Loving heavenly Father, remove from my system every trace of jealousy, and help me to rejoice in the joy of all Your children. Amen.

'Dear brother Paul …'

FOR READING AND MEDITATION
2 PETER 3:8–18

'… our Lord's patience means salvation, just as our dear brother Paul also wrote to you …' (v.15)

Jealousy begins with a wrong comparison. We compare ourselves with others instead of with Jesus. We saw that in the last recorded conversation between Jesus and Peter, Peter was caught up in a little lingering jealousy. He had his face John-ward instead of Jesus-ward. Frequently I have wondered how Peter overcame his tendency to jealousy. How did he deal with the emergence of Paul, for example, on the apostolic scene? We are not told how Peter reacted either to Paul's great appeal and ministry, but when we read Peter's two epistles we get a picture of a man whose face was turned completely towards Jesus. No hint of a lingering jealousy here. Had the fires of Pentecost burned it out? I believe they had.

O Father, if the flames of jealousy arise in my heart, overpower them, I pray, with Your living fire. In Christ's name I ask it. Amen.

'Near Me ... near the fire'

FOR READING AND MEDITATION
LUKE 24:13–35

*'Were not our hearts burning within us while he talked
with us on the road ...?' (v.32)*

It is to the fire-baptising Christ that we must turn
if we are to be rid of jealousy. His fire is the most
powerful, the most intense, and the most refining flame
the universe knows. It burns through jealousy like acid
through paper. Put all your jealousies in His hands. He
can do with them what you cannot do. There is a saying
attributed to Jesus which, though not found in the Bible,
nevertheless has the ring of reality about it: 'He that is
near Me is near the fire.' How could this be otherwise
when Jesus is God, and 'God is a consuming fire' (Heb.
12:29)? *Get close to Jesus.* When you get close to Him
you will soon feel the effects of His glorious energy and
cleansing flame.

*Lord Jesus, as I take a step closer to You now, please take a
step closer to me. Let me feel the effects of Your fire. Amen.*

The final battle

FOR READING AND MEDITATION
HEBREWS 13:1–6

'Keep your lives free from the love of money and be content with what you have …' (v.5)

How can the flames of the Spirit overpower the spirit of acquisitiveness? I turn again to the note I have been striking day after day – the note of surrender. I turn to it for it is the turntable on which life turns from materialisation to spiritualisation. The material must be surrendered to God or we will surrender to the material. Please keep in mind the fact that I am not talking about the fire of God burning up possessions but the *love* of possessions. Money can become a master or a means of doing good. If not surrendered to God, it is a master – a terrible master. Only men and women who are touched by Christ can overcome the raging fire of acquisitiveness once it begins to burn in their heart.

Lord Jesus Christ, help me to take all my possessions and make them the instruments of Your purposes. Amen.

'Minted personality'

FOR READING AND MEDITATION
MATTHEW 13:18–23

'… the worries of this life and the deceitfulness of wealth choke [the word], making it unfruitful.' (v.22)

James Moffatt translates today's verse in this way: 'the delight of being rich'; that is, wealth as an end in itself rather than in what it can do. We cannot serve God and money, we can serve God *with* money. When the fire of God is allowed to fall on the altar of our heart, and the acquisitive desire is burned up, then life takes on a sense of stewardship. We feel we are handling our money on behalf of Another. That does something to the whole of life – it puts sacredness into the secular. A minister friend of mine refers to money as 'minted personality'. He is right. When given to God and used by Him it is just as sacred as the words uttered in the pulpit. Both speak the same message – and equally.

Lord Jesus Christ, may I regard myself as Your steward, and serve You with the money You have entrusted to me. Amen.

Gold seekers – or God seekers?

FOR READING AND MEDITATION
1 PETER 5:1–11

'Be shepherds ... as God wants you to be; not greedy for money, but eager to serve ...' (v.2)

Some of you may have many possessions and wealth. You do not have to get rid of your possessions in order to be a dedicated Christian; you do need, however, to bring them under God's stewardship. The flame of His Spirit must be allowed to burn away all self-interest. Enjoy material possessions and use them, but watch them, for unguarded they can consume your life. Two groups of American pioneers trekked west. One group had written on their wagons 'Gold seekers'; the other group had written 'God seekers'. One group dissipated whilst the other group founded a community. Are you a gold seeker or a God seeker? Has the divine fire consumed all the acquisitive desires in your heart? If not, why not?

O Father, may I not set my heart on things that will pass away but on what will last for all eternity. In Jesus' name I ask it. Amen.

'It all depends on the liver!'

FOR READING AND MEDITATION
PHILIPPIANS 1:12–26

'For to me, to live is Christ and to die is gain.' (v.21)

When William James, the psychologist, was asked, 'Is life worth living?' he answered wittily, 'That depends on the liver!' The ambiguity implied that for life to be worth living one had to be without any physical complaints. Paul endured a great amount of physical discomfort after he became a Christian. He wrote, 'I have ... been in prison ... in danger in the city, in danger in the country ... have often gone without sleep; I have known hunger and thirst and have often gone without food; I have been cold and naked' (2 Cor. 11:23–27). Yet he lived a full and robust life. Why? Because he did not live for pleasure. His heart was set on fire by Jesus Christ. A living interest worked within him – Christ.

Lord Jesus, set my heart on fire with Your zeal, Your power and Your passion. For Your honour and glory I pray. Amen.

Our greetest hunger

FOR READING AND MEDITATION
ECCLESIASTES 3:1–15

'He has also set eternity in the hearts of men ...' (v.11)

M any think our greatest hunger is for pleasure
but they fail to understand that deep down it is
really the hunger for God. God has set eternity in our
hearts. Augustine expressed the same thought in his
well-known prayer: 'O God, our hearts are restless and
they cannot find rest until they find it in Thee.' Let me
reiterate that there is nothing wrong with experiencing
pleasure. The wrong comes when we allow ourselves to
be consumed by it – when we live for it alone. It is God,
we are reminded, who 'richly provides us with everything
for our enjoyment' (1 Tim. 6:17). The desire for pleasure
is transformed by the heavenly flame. It is still there,
but it is caught up in a higher and more consuming
passion.

*Father, I know that in my heart there is a desire to experience
pleasure but please bring it under Your complete control. In
Jesus' name I ask it. Amen.*

'Hasn't he changed!'

FOR READING AND MEDITATION
GALATIANS 2:11–21

'… I no longer live, but Christ lives in me.' (v.20)

The roots of hedonism – the self-interested pursuit of pleasure for its own sake – lie in inner emptiness and boredom. One man who spent a week in Soho experiencing every earthly pleasure confessed to being bored with his life. I invited him to repent of his former lifestyle and receive Christ, which he did. Within days he was filled with the Spirit and went back to Soho to share Christ with the very prostitutes he had spent his time with. I heard one person say of him, 'My, hasn't he *changed!*' He had been consumed by a love for Christ. He had been burning before, but burning with the wrong kind of flame. Now he burned with love for Christ – a different and infinitely more powerful fire.

Father, immerse me in the heavenly flame so that I will burn, not with self-interest, but with God-interest. In Jesus' name. Amen.

Making our hearts a hearth

FOR READING AND MEDITATION
ISAIAH 66:5–16

'See, the Lord is coming with fire ...' (v.15)

In the UK some decades ago the get-rich-quick purveyors of pornography persuaded a number of befuddled politicians that it was necessary to relax the laws governing this issue. Evidence is now being brought to show that pornography on the internet and in magazines has a direct influence on the increasing sexual addictions and violence we are witnessing in our society. Why were people able to open the floodgates to this evil? Perhaps the reason why this destructive fire rages so fiercely in contemporary society is not because the divine fire is unable to extinguish it, but because so few Christians are ready to allow their heart to become a hearth in which it can burn and oppose such godlessness.

O God, make my heart a hearth on which Your fire might burn continuously. I ask this in and through Christ, my Saviour and Lord. Amen.

Facts – on fire

FOR READING AND MEDITATION
MARK 16:9–20

'Then the disciples ... preached everywhere, and the Lord worked with them and confirmed his word by the signs that accompanied it.' (v.20)

Our power and influence is in direct proportion to the degree with which we are filled with the holy heavenly fire. So many of us lack passion. We attempt to meet the passionate arguments of the libertarians with cold logic, forgetting that it is only as ideas are presented with enthusiasm and energy that they have impact and power. Facts are good, logic is good, but the facts and the logic must be set on fire by the Holy Spirit. The disciples had all the facts of the gospel prior to Pentecost. But immediately after the resurrection we find that they were behind closed doors for fear of the Jews (see John 20:19)! Then came Pentecost and suddenly the facts were set on fire. After that – what a difference!

O God, I am grateful for all the facts that build my faith, but I pray that the Holy Spirit will kindle a flame of love in my heart. Amen.

'The worst form of blasphemy'

FOR READING AND MEDITATION
REVELATION 3:14–22

'He who has an ear, let him hear what the Spirit says to the churches.' (v.22)

I once met a man whose job was to go around different churches insuring them against fire. I told him I was praying that more and more churches would catch fire! Facetious? Yes, but he saw my point. There are far too many fire-proof churches in Christendom. The Laodiceans were lukewarm believers and so Christ warned them that unless they became zealous and got on fire He would 'spit' them out of His mouth (v.16). And, in the opinion of Dr G. Campbell Morgan, 'Lukewarmness is the worst form of blasphemy'. Our Lord did not say that He would spit anyone out of His mouth for being too hot. Our zeal is a response to the amazing love Christ has for us. Whatever you do, don't be lukewarm.

O God, we repent of the indifference that has crept into our lives. Lord, in Your mercy, forgive us, and send Your Spirit to revive us we pray. Amen.

'Fiery Christianity'

FOR READING AND MEDITATION
JAMES 5:13–20

'Whoever turns a sinner from the error of his way will save him from death and cover over a multitude of sins.' (v.20)

Carol Santiago was a New York girl who, on a visit to the Philippines, became consumed with communism. Her husband was killed and she was left alone with two small children. A Christian couple took her into their home and it was there that she came across what she called 'fiery Christianity'. At first she was contemptuous of the couple's prayers, worship and Bible reading. But one day, when her little child was ill, the couple prayed and the child was instantly healed. Now Carol is busy bringing others to Christ. If people ask her why she does things that as a communist she would have despised, she remembers that Christian home where she saw warm, outgoing love in action. Again: redeemed from fire by fire!

O Father, may my fire set some other heart on fire with love for You. In Christ's name I ask it. Amen.

'A righteous fire'

FOR READING AND MEDITATION
ISAIAH 30:27–33

*'The Lord will cause men to hear his majestic voice ...
with ... consuming fire ...' (v.30)*

Fanaticism can lead people to sacrifice truth, justice, honour, virtue and the moral law if these things stand in the way of their cause – even going as far as to kill and destroy. But this is not the case with those who are on fire with the Holy Spirit. Christ calls us to fiery discipleship, but not to extreme fanaticism. I asked one such person now converted to Christ, 'What's the difference between the fire that burns in your heart now and the fire that once consumed you?' He thought for a few moments and then said, 'The fire of God is in harmony with all the principles of the universe; it is a righteous fire.' God's fire burns against evil but at the same time honours all that is righteous and true.

Father, You inflame me not merely with zeal for a cause, but with zeal for all that is virtuous and true. I am so grateful. Amen.

'To and for Him'

FOR READING AND MEDITATION
LEVITICUS 6:8–13

*'The fire must be kept burning on the altar continuously;
it must not go out.' (v.13)*

Paul wrote, '… we are of the opinion and conviction that if One died for all, then all died; and He died for all, so that all those who live might live no longer to and for themselves, but to and for Him Who died and was raised again for their sake' (2 Cor. 5:14–15, Amplified). Notice the phrase *'to and for Him'*. There you have the secret of impassioned and energetic living: 'to and for Him'. Christ's cross becomes the altar of our soul where the fire never goes out, as it never went out in the Holy of Holies in the Temple in Jerusalem (Lev. 24:1–4). Your life becomes 'To and for Him'. The true fire, the heavenly fire, is the fire of deep devotion to Jesus Christ.

Father, may the flame of devotion You have kindled in my heart continually rise upwards in praise and adoration. In Jesus' name. Amen.

Honest to God

FOR READING AND MEDITATION
PSALM 51:1–13

'Surely you desire truth in the inner parts; you teach me wisdom in the inmost place.' (v.6)

How then do we experience God's fire for ourselves? *First be absolutely honest with yourself.* Maybe you are religious but have never had a personal encounter with Jesus. It may be that you have been drawn to the Christian faith but are not consumed by it, that Christ has never been admitted into your life. I urge you, as soon as you have finished today's reading, to bow your head wherever you are and invite Christ into your life as Saviour and Lord. On the other hand, you may be a committed disciple of Christ but with no fire in your heart. Take a moment now to honestly appraise your spiritual life and ask, 'Is my life more like a dull habit or an acute fever?'

O Father, help me to be honest. There are fears within me that cause me to draw back, but deep down I want to be truly Yours. Amen.

The road to recovery

FOR READING AND MEDITATION
REVELATION 2:1–7

'Remember the height from which you have fallen! Repent and do the things you did at first.' (v.5)

I f in yesterday's moments of honesty you felt that your spiritual life needs to be set aflame, then the next step is that of *repentance*. Believe me, when we come short of what God expects and provides for our spiritual lives, the issue is usually ours – not His. We need to repent – repent of our lack of trust – and confess that we have been attempting to hold our lives together in our own strength instead of depending on Christ and the Holy Spirit. When the church at Ephesus left their first love, our Lord showed them the way back: remember, repent and return. I appeal to you to join in this prayer of confession and repentance.

O Father, forgive me that I have depended on myself instead of on You. I confess that I prefer self-sufficiency to trusting You. Right now I repent of that and turn to You afresh – please meet me afresh. In Christ's name I ask it. Amen.

We are coming to a King

FOR READING AND MEDITATION
LUKE 11:1–13

'… how much more will your Father in heaven give the Holy Spirit to those who ask him!' (v.13)

We are ready now to take the next step, which is recognising that *giving good gifts to His children is the thing God most enjoys doing.* A parent desires to bestow nothing but the best upon his child, and so it is with God. A parent loves to give their children something they long for and that is good for them. At such times joy rises up and overflows. It is the same with God. He is more eager to give you the Holy Spirit in all His fullness than you are to receive Him. It is terribly important for you to understand this eagerness of God to give, for if you have doubts about it, you will not come to Him in confidence. Your asking will be short-circuited from the start.

Lord, I believe John's words: 'This is the confidence we have in approaching God: that if we ask anything according to his will, he hears us' (1 John 5:14). Amen.

'Where is this place?'

FOR READING AND MEDITATION
JOHN 7:25–39

'… Jesus … said in a loud voice, "If anyone is thirsty,
let him come to me and drink."' (v.37)

God not only wants to give, but *waits* to give. Some
of God's gifts are given whether or not people ask
for them – the sunshine and the rain being two examples
(see Matthew 5:45). Not so the Holy Spirit. Before He
is given there must be a real desire to receive Him. One
preacher led a man on a long walk to be filled with the
Spirit until at last the man said, 'Listen, I can't bear this
any longer. I've got to have a meeting with God. I want
my life to be set on fire by the Holy Spirit. I must have
this experience now.' The friend responded, 'This is the
place right here.' So together they knelt and right there,
where the man had come to the point of desperation, he
received his personal Pentecost.

*Lord, You said, 'Blessed are those who hunger and thirst …
for they will be filled.' I hunger and thirst for more of You.
Please fill me now. Amen.*

A prayer for power

FOR READING AND MEDITATION
ACTS 4:23–31

'After they prayed, the place where they were meeting was shaken. And they were all filled with the Holy Spirit ...'
(v.31)

What else do we need to do in order to draw near to Christ and have our lives set on fire by the Holy Spirit? We must *pray*. To receive, we must ask. I include here part of a prayer thousands have found to be a powerful catalyst and inspiration in their seeking after God:

'Lord, end this wishy-washy, lukewarm, mumbling religion and set us on fire. Put the divine fire in us before the demonic fires destroy us and our world. Do not spew us out of Your mouth, but set us on fire. God of courage, sweep aside our pitiful timidity. Help Christendom to rise in deeds and in fire and in truth; change our defeat into glorious victory. Give us a Pentecost at any cost. Send a Pentecost right now and begin it in me. Keep Your promise, Lord Jesus Christ, and baptise us with the Holy Spirit and with fire. The altar is ready, the offering is laid. Now, Lord, send the fire.' Amen.

Maintaining the glow

FOR READING AND MEDITATION
MATTHEW 9:27–38

'According to your faith will it be done to you ...' (v.29)

It is one thing to be set on fire, it is another to maintain that fire. Sadly, many Christians who were once Christ's incendiaries have allowed the fire to die down and have become, 'icily conformist and splendidly dull'. What should we do to maintain the glow of God at the centre of our soul? I must bring you back once again to the word *trust*. We must recognise that the divine fire is not ours to create, but is ours to receive. It means taking God at His Word: *According to your faith will it be done to you.* Once you have opened your life to Him, and all sin has been put aside, then you must believe that He is now at work in you. Believe it — and as faith takes hold the fire will burn.

Father, I ask not only that the divine fire will burn within me but that it will go on burning in me. Keep it burning; keep me burning. Amen.

'Lips only too ready'

FOR READING AND MEDITATION
JOHN 4:27–38

'I tell you, open your eyes and look at the fields! They are ripe for harvest.' (v.35)

Another thing we must do to keep the fire burning on the altar of our lives is to *share with others what Christ has done for us*. Sam Shoemaker said, 'If it were true that the ego had been brought up under the cross, and nailed there with Christ, we should come away with our hearts on fire and our faces shining and our lips only too ready to make known the wonders of his grace.' There you have it: 'lips only too ready'. The nature of fire is to increase – to extend itself. Show me someone who is on fire for Christ and I will show you someone who does everything he or she can do to bring others to the faith. And if you don't go with the fire then you damp it down, and it will soon stop burning.

O Father, help us not to fail future generations by keeping the fire to ourselves – give us 'lips only too ready'. Amen.

What is fire-lighted evangelism?

FOR READING AND MEDITATION
1 PETER 3:8–16

'Always be prepared to give an answer to everyone who asks you to give the reason for the hope that you have.' (v.15)

L et us make sure we don't fall into the trap of thinking that evangelism is something confined to crowded halls or arenas. Fiery discipleship is not typified by shouting 'Jesus saves' or pushing gospel leaflets into people's hands. It involves entering into the lives of those with whom we relate day after day after day. It means laughing with them as well as praying for them, crying with them as well as inviting them to church, going out of our way to let them know we care for them as individuals as well as putting their names on a prayer list. There will be failures, but there will be victories, too – victories that timid, unimaginative, complacent Christians will never, never win!

O God, burn so powerfully in me that all those with whom I come in contact will recognise there is something different about me. Amen.

More fire!

FOR READING AND MEDITATION
LUKE 3:7–18

'He will baptise you with the Holy Spirit and with fire.' (v.16)

Permit me to summarise. There are two kinds of fire in this universe: one divine, the other destructive. T.S. Eliot said that we only live, only 'suspire, consumed by either fire or fire'. This is why there must be more fire in our church services, more fire in our prayer meetings, more fire in our pulpits, more fire in our family devotions, more fire in our evangelistic outreach, more fire in our missionary support, more fire in our community involvement, more fire in our fight against poverty, immorality and permissiveness. Fire! More fire! Christ's kind of fire – for our intellect, emotions and will, for our homes, our churches, our businesses, and for all the nations of the world!

Lord, I ask You to baptise me with the Holy Spirit and with fire. May I burn with a new passion and boldness for You. Amen and Amen.

Wise up and live

FOR READING AND MEDITATION
PROVERBS 1:1-19

'... for attaining wisdom and discipline; for understanding words of insight ...' (v.2)

O ver the next two months we set out to explore some of the great and thrilling themes of the book of Proverbs. What is the purpose of Proverbs? Our text for today gives us the clue. Listen to how the Living Bible paraphrases it: 'He [Solomon] wrote them to teach his people how to live – how to act in every circumstance ...' This, then, is what Proverbs is all about – wisdom for living. Millions of people know how to make a living but do not know how to live. They know everything about life except how to live it. I tell you, the more you understand the book of Proverbs, and the more you put its truths and principles into practice, the more effective will be your living. I guarantee it.

O Father, help me come to grips with the wisdom that enables me not just to live, but to live abundantly. Amen.

Wisdom personified

FOR READING AND MEDITATION
PROVERBS 1:20–33

'… but whoever listens to me will live in safety and be at ease, without fear of harm.' (v.33)

You will not get far when reading Proverbs before you begin to notice that both wisdom and its opposite, foolishness, are personified as women – Lady Wisdom and Lady Folly – each of whom attempts to persuade people to follow her ways. We use a similar form of expression when we personify natural laws and poetically refer to them as 'Mother Nature'. The purpose of this personification in Proverbs is to make the reader vividly aware that over and against the fatal attraction of folly, wisdom brings security and contentment. Wisdom is the soul's true bride and true counsellor. Wisdom is good for us; it is what our personalities were designed for by God Himself.

O Father, help me to grasp the truth that I am made for a certain way of living – Your way of wisdom and not the world's way of foolishness. Amen.

The source of all wisdom

FOR READING AND MEDITATION
PROVERBS 2:12–22

'Wisdom will save you from the ways of wicked men ...'
(v.12)

Many commentators are agreed that the personification of wisdom in Proverbs prepares the way for Paul's great statement in I Corinthians 1:24, that Christ is 'the power of God and the wisdom of God'. If so, then it suggests Proverbs is not simply a set of guidelines for our lives, but it hints that true wisdom lies in a Person – Jesus Christ. The Christian message moves beyond the wise proverbs of Solomon, which commend themselves to non-Christians as well as Christians, and points to the fact that the highest wisdom comes from a relationship with the One who is the fount of all wisdom – Jesus. Knowing the principles of wisdom is one thing; knowing the Person in whom all wisdom resides is another.

O Father, how can I sufficiently thank You that by faith I am linked to the source of all wisdom – the Lord Jesus Christ? Amen.

Sophomores – 'wise fools'

FOR READING AND MEDITATION
PROVERBS 4:1–9

'Do not forsake wisdom, and she will protect you; love her, and she will watch over you.' (v.6)

Knowledge and wisdom are different. Knowledge is the capacity to comprehend and retain what we are taught; wisdom is the ability to put that knowledge to best effect. In the USA a second year student is called a 'sophomore', a term derived from the Greek words for 'wise' and 'foolish' – in other words, a 'wise fool'. How revealing! When we reach the higher stages of education we think that we know it all, but really we are still a fool. A 'fool' in Proverbs is not someone who can't pass a simple literacy or numeracy test; he or she is someone who thinks they know what life is all about but does not. Those whom the world recognises as 'wise' may, from heaven's standpoint, be the biggest fools.

Father, my lifestyle may appear foolish to those around me, but if I am following Your principles it is the highest wisdom. Amen.

The 'wisdom literature'

FOR READING AND MEDITATION
PROVERBS 5:15–23

'For a man's ways are in full view of the LORD, and he examines all his paths.' (v.21)

The Old Testament consists of three sections: first, the Law, second, the Prophets, and third, the Writings – answering to the three groups of leaders outlined in Jeremiah 18:18: '... for the teaching of the law by the *priest* will not be lost, nor will counsel from the *wise*, nor the word from the *prophets*.' Included within the category of the Writings are the wisdom books – Job, Psalms, Proverbs, Ecclesiastes and Song of Songs. The book of Proverbs is crammed with the best advice it is possible to obtain, and it is a tragedy that it is not part of our own educational system because the world was designed for wisdom, and those who followed wisdom would find that the world was made for them.

Gracious Father, help me develop a love for Your wisdom literature and grant that new evidences of Your wisdom may be seen in my life. Amen.

'Portable medicine'

FOR READING AND MEDITATION
PROVERBS 28:1–17

'… *a man of understanding and knowledge maintains order.' (v.2)*

Alexander Maclaren, a famous preacher from a past generation, said, 'Proverbs is portable medicine for the fevers of youth.' How true. And, as with any medicine, what matters is that you take it whether or not you know the doctor who prescribed it. A number of young men and women known to me have told me that they came to faith in Jesus Christ through reading the book of Proverbs. One said to me, 'When I applied the principles of Proverbs, and saw that these wise and witty sayings really worked, I was drawn to search for the One whose hand was so clearly present in the book and also in my life. After reading the instruction manual I wanted to know the Instructor.'

O Father, help me use any influence I have with the young to motivate them to read and absorb what is found in the book of Proverbs. Amen.

'Invoked or not ...'

FOR READING AND MEDITATION
PROVERBS 8:12–36

'Blessed is the man who listens to me, watching daily at my doors ...' (v.34)

The more you read Proverbs, and the more you apply its words to your life, the more you will find that its wise and witty sayings 'work'. They work because God has set things up to work this way. It was said of Carl Jung, the famous psychologist, that written over his study door were these words: 'Invoked or not, God is present.' This interesting statement provides us with a clue to understanding Proverbs, for whether or not men and women invoke the Creator, His creative and sustaining wisdom goes on giving them a world where wisdom operates and where things make sense to humankind. It has to be said that life on earth would be a great deal better if the wisdom of Proverbs, rather than folly, prevailed.

Father, Your love reaches down to help people live life in a sensible way even though they may never know You personally. Amen.

'Come into my house'

FOR READING AND MEDITATION
PROVERBS 9:1–9

'Wisdom has built her house; she has hewn out its seven pillars.' (v.1)

Our text for today tells us that wisdom is like a house built on seven pillars. There are two main ways of interpreting this verse. One view is that both wisdom and folly have a house to which humankind is invited. Wisdom has a much larger house than folly, being built upon 'seven pillars' – a sign in ancient times of wealth, status and prestige. There is no doubt that this interpretation of the text has much to commend it, but it is the other view that I am following in these studies – namely that wisdom has seven major aspects. So my intention is to give you what I consider to be the seven chief aspects of wisdom. We need wisdom to live – and the book of Proverbs will give it to us.

Father, grant that as I expose myself to the truths of Your Word, wisdom may become more deeply imprinted upon my spirit. In Jesus' name I pray. Amen.

The ability to trust

FOR READING AND MEDITATION
PROVERBS 3:1–18

'Trust in the Lord with all your heart and lean not on your own understanding ...' (v.5)

Consider the first of the seven pillars on which I believe wisdom is built – *trust*. A dictionary says trust is 'a firm belief in the reliability, honesty, veracity, justice and strength of a person or thing'. Trust is confidence – confidence that what we believe about a person or thing is true. We tend to think of trust as being a spiritual quality, but actually it is an essential part of life for everyone. It would be very difficult to get through a single day without the exercise of trust. All government, all economics, all institutions, all marriages, and all relationships between people are fundamentally governed by trust. We cannot relate well to God or others unless we have the ability to trust.

Father, I see that trust is an essential thread that runs through the whole of life. Teach me the art of trusting, for an art it is. Help me to maintain complete confidence in You. Amen.

Trust is good for us

FOR READING AND MEDITATION
PROVERBS 14:14–26

'A simple man believes anything, but a prudent man gives thought to his steps.' (v.15)

Without trust, society would deteriorate into paranoia – the feeling that everyone is out to get you. Mental health specialists see an inability to trust as a symptom of emotional ill health, and conditions such as chronic anxiety, nervousness or paranoia could be caused by an inability to trust. We must learn how to trust while at the same time exercising a certain amount of caution. Today's text tells us that 'a simple man believes anything'. However, that should not cause us to go to the other extreme and believe that everything people tell us is a lie or a fabrication. The point is that we should not be gullible. Truth is a narrow column and we must watch that we do not lose our balance and fall off.

O Father, help me to be a balanced person – one who stands on the narrow column of truth without falling off into one extreme or the other. Amen.

A snake in the grass

FOR READING AND MEDITATION
PROVERBS 16:10–20

'... *blessed is he who trusts in the Lord.' (v.20)*

We live in a fallen world. God made the first human pair perfect in every way, and put them in a beautiful garden. They trusted Him for everything they needed and not once did He let them down. However, there was a 'snake in the grass' that brought mistrust of God and of each other. In one way or another the Fall has played havoc with this issue of trust, but we must be careful that we do not allow the failures of trust we may experience on the human level to affect our view of God. Let me spell it out as clearly as I can: you can put your trust in God without fear of ever being let down. Whoever else you may not be able to trust – you can trust your heavenly Father.

O Father, what encouragement this thought gives me: whoever else I cannot trust, I can trust You. Amen.

Why is trust difficult?

FOR READING AND MEDITATION
PROVERBS 28:18–28

'He who trusts in himself is a fool, but he who walks in wisdom is kept safe.' (v.26)

Why do some people find it so difficult to trust? Trust is a learned response, and we begin learning it the moment we are born. A newborn baby arrives in the world with a great deal of vulnerability, and among other things has to learn the art of developing a basic trust. My counselling experience has shown that people with an inability to trust are usually those who experienced serious privation, abuse or cruelty in their early years, especially from their parents. This is no reason to despair, however, for when we have faith in Jesus Christ we become children of God – we have a new parent and a new parentage. And He enables us to overcome whatever difficulties there may have been in our past.

Father, may my focus not be on what has been but on what can be, and on what will be when I am rightly related to You. Amen.

How to forgive

FOR READING AND MEDITATION
PROVERBS 30:21–33

'… *as twisting the nose produces blood, so stirring up anger produces strife.*' (v.33)

How do we overcome the problem of a lack of trust? The first thing we must do is demonstrate a willingness to forgive those who deprived us, hurt us or betrayed us. It can be hard, but not impossible. Some say, 'My problem is that I can't forgive,' I have usually responded by saying, 'No, that's not your problem. Your problem is that you don't know how much you have been forgiven.' Because Jesus Christ died on the cross for our sins, God has forgiven us, pardoned us and bestowed upon us His royal favour. Having been given such forgiveness can we, dare we, withhold it from anyone who has hurt us or betrayed our trust, no matter how awful or painful that hurt has been?

Father, Your Word is frank and open; help me to respond to it in the same way and help me forgive as I have been forgiven. Amen.

My way – or God's way

FOR READING AND MEDITATION
PROVERBS 14:1–13

'There is a way that seems right to a man, but in the end it leads to death.' (v.12)

The second step to overcoming lack of trust is the recognition that, having been let down by others, we have determined in our hearts that we will never trust another person again. The determination never to trust another person again may be a human reaction, but it is not God's way. The Christian faith is all about relating to people. We must therefore bring this self-protective determination to preserve our own soul before God in an act of repentance, and indicate by an act of resolve that no matter how others may treat us, we will confidently place our trust in Him. We decide that we can trust God to hold us when we relate to others, irrespective of whether we are accepted or rejected or let down.

O Father, the determination to stay safe seems so right, yet it is so wrong. I turn from my way to Your way. Hold me secure. Amen.

Is trust idealistic?

FOR READING AND MEDITATION
PROVERBS 29:19–27

'Fear of man will prove to be a snare, but whoever trusts in the Lord is kept safe.' (v.25)

Sometimes someone has said to me 'Isn't it idealistic to expect me to be vulnerable to further hurt after I have been let down and betrayed?' My answer is to point them to Jesus. If He can do it then so can we – if we depend on His strength and not ours. Jesus knows better than anyone what it means to be let down and betrayed. After Peter had betrayed Him, Jesus did not allow the hurt He felt to deter Him from continuing, even pursuing, the relationship (John 21:15–17). *That's* what I mean by vulnerability. *That's* what I mean by love. Jesus' openness with Peter opened up again the possibility of relationship and also opened up the way for Peter to enter into an important new role within the fledgling Church.

Father, You can make me so secure that I, too, am able to be vulnerable in my relationships. Help me to demonstrate it. In Jesus' name. Amen.

'Yours trustingly'

FOR READING AND MEDITATION
PROVERBS 11:25–31

'Whoever trusts in his riches will fall ...' (v.28)

God does not promise to keep us from being hurt in our relationships, but He does promise to keep us from being destroyed. The more you trust in God, the more effective you will be in your relationships with others. Because your ultimate trust is in God you will be free from unconscious manipulative or exploitative techniques and, drawing your security from Him, you can give yourself more freely to others. 'Love does not begin,' someone has said, 'until you expect nothing in return.' When your trust is wholly and fully in the Lord Jesus you can love like that. Decide now to put in God's hands all the hurts, traumas and betrayals of the past. Forgive all those who have let you down. Give God all your trust.

O God, break down any last barrier that may be hindering me from putting my trust fully in You. Help me begin and end every day by saying, 'Yours trustingly'. Amen.

Integrity – 'profound wisdom'

FOR READING AND MEDITATION
PROVERBS 10:9–17

'The man of integrity walks securely, but he who takes crooked paths will be found out.' (v.9)

I consider the second pillar of wisdom to be – *integrity*. The dictionary defines integrity as: 'wholeness, soundness, trustworthiness, uprightness, honesty'. One of the mistakes people make when thinking about wisdom is to confuse it with learning, intelligence, brilliance or cleverness. Many clever professionals have a great deal of knowledge but lack wisdom. For example, the marriage counsellor who can't hold his own marriage together; the psychiatrist who slides into depression; the economist who goes bankrupt playing the stock market; the church leader who leaves his family for another woman, and so on. Knowledge is important, but integrity is a profound wisdom in the art of living.

O God, give me in addition to trust a high degree of integrity. I want not only to trust others but I want them to trust me. In Jesus' name. Amen.

'I would rather be right ...'

FOR READING AND MEDITATION
PROVERBS 8:1–11

'... for wisdom is more precious than rubies, and nothing you desire can compare with her.' (v.11)

Charles Spurgeon wrote to the then Prime Minister of Britain, William Gladstone, in these words: 'We believe in no man's infallibility but it is restful to be sure of one man's integrity.' What makes us so suspicious of politicians, even though politics can be a noble profession, is not that they might make mistakes, but that sometimes staying in office is more important to them than honour and candour. Henry Clay, when about to introduce to the American Congress a bill that was heavily weighted in favour of morality, was told, 'If you do this, it will kill your chances of becoming president.' His reply was, 'I would rather be right than be president.'

Father, I see that the reason I am not wiser is that I do not have enough of You. Please fill me with Your Spirit. Amen.

'A lie has short legs'

FOR READING AND MEDITATION
PROVERBS 28:18–28

'He whose walk is blameless is kept safe, but he whose ways are perverse will suddenly fall.' (v.18)

We and the universe are made for integrity. Will the universe sustain a lie? I have no hesitation in saying that it will not for I believe that the universe is not built for the success of a lie. The Tamils in South India have a saying that goes like this: 'The life of the cleverest lie is only eight days.' A lie may not break itself upon the universe today or tomorrow, but one day it will. Before World War II the Germans used to say, 'Lies have short legs', meaning that they were bad in the long run. During the war that saying was changed to 'Lies have one short leg'. Why? Because Goebbels, the propaganda minister, had one short leg! In God's moral universe nobody gets away with anything.

Father, help me to be a person of integrity and truth, and thus get results, not consequences. In Jesus' name. Amen.

Can a lie be justified?

FOR READING AND MEDITATION
PROVERBS 19:1–9

'… he who pours out lies will perish.' (v.9)

Contemporary society is increasingly facing and needing to deal with 'situational ethics', which would have us believe that sometimes, under certain situations, a lie is admissible. I think that is a dangerous and deadly path. A lie is never right – no matter what attempts we might make to justify it. 'God is not a man, that he should lie', we are told in Numbers 23:19, and in 1 John 2:21 we read, '… no lie comes from the truth'. To justify lying in some situations is the argument, 'This is what we must and ought to do because it makes sense'. But once we view sin as a 'must' and as an 'ought' it is magically turned into something that is 'good' and 'right' when truly it is 'bad' and 'wrong'.

O Father, in a world that seems to be always looking for excuses and exceptions, help me to conform to Your rules. In Jesus' name. Amen.

Two important facts

FOR READING AND MEDITATION
PROVERBS 6:12–19

'There are six things the LORD hates … a false witness who pours out lies …' (vv.16,19)

A Christian view of ethics rejects every scenario which situational ethics advances if it fails to recognise two important biblical facts. First, *God's sovereignty*. God will always prepare a way out for His people (1 Cor. 10:13). Second, *the Holy Spirit's power*. The believer is encouraged not to worry about what he or she has to say in difficult situations. Jesus has promised, 'At that time you will be given what to say, for it will not be you speaking, but the Spirit of your Father …' (Matt. 10:19–20). Those who try to excuse the breaking of any of God's moral laws on the pretext that it feels 'right' or seems 'good' sow the seeds of disruption in their own inner being. It is not the way of wisdom.

Father, help us to trust Your Word even when it runs counter to our own feelings. In Jesus' name we pray. Amen.

Dishonesty is doomed

FOR READING AND MEDITATION
PROVERBS 14:1–13

*'A truthful witness does not deceive, but a false witness
pours out lies.' (v.5)*

Something dies the moment you are dishonest or fail to
be a person of integrity. Self-respect dies within you.
Degeneration begins to damage your heart the moment
dishonesty enters it. You are not so much punished for
your sin as by your sin. A milkman in India had to drive
his cow and calf from door to door in the hot sun and
milk the cow in the presence of each housewife. You see,
he was discovered putting water in the milk and now,
because he couldn't be trusted, he had to milk the cow
before the eyes of everyone he served. The milkman's
dishonesty doomed him to drudgery. The moral universe
had the last word. I am made for the wisdom of integrity
and I will not function well without it.

*O Father, help me grasp this simple but important fact –
that I am designed for truth and honesty. Amen.*

Truth is truth is truth

FOR READING AND MEDITATION
PROVERBS 30:1–9

'Keep falsehood and lies far from me ...' (v.8)

When a successful businessman was asked for the greatest need in his sphere of business he said, 'Integrity. Almost daily I am faced with dishonesty and duplicity, and whenever I confront it people take the view that dishonesty is only a problem when it is found out.' But this hinders business. Likewise, Christians who lack integrity hinder the progress of the gospel in this world and set Christ's message in a false light. Determine to be honest in thought and speech and act. Lay this down as a cornerstone of your life, especially you who are young, and begin building from there. Whatever you do, shun like a plague the temptations of situational ethics and admit no exceptions. Truth is truth is truth.

O God, if I run from truth I run from myself, for I am made for truth. Keep me true, dear Lord. In Jesus' name. Amen.

Self-exploratory surgery

FOR READING AND MEDITATION
PROVERBS 23:15–25

'Buy the truth and do not sell it; get wisdom, discipline and understanding.' (v.23)

Today I invite you to undertake some self exploratory surgery of the soul. This is not just an interesting idea, it is something we are required to do because Scripture commands it: 'But let a man examine himself' (I Cor. 11:28, NKJV). Right now, in God's presence, ask yourself: Am I honest? Am I a person of integrity? Can my word be trusted? Remember, only you can perform this surgery on your soul – only you. No one else but you knows the truth about yourself. You can rationalise and twist the facts and no one will know the difference – except you. And remember, too, that there can be no wisdom without morality, no expertise in living without truth and honesty. The wise are those who have integrity.

Father, by Your Word, and through Your Spirit, right now cut away in me all that is untrue and dishonest. For Jesus' sake. Amen.

Take another path

FOR READING AND MEDITATION
PROVERBS 5:1-14

'Keep to a path far from her ...' (v.8)

I believe the third pillar of wisdom to be – *personal purity*. We live in an age that largely ignores the biblical teaching to keep sexual intercourse until marriage. Even some sections of the Church now accept the 'new morality' but I have no hesitation in rejecting this, both as not biblical and anti-relationship. The emphasis of Proverbs at this point is to avoid putting yourself in a position of temptation – to keep well away from the danger of seduction. A man once went to the great American preacher D.L. Moody with a tale of personal moral disaster and said, 'Now, Mr Moody, what would you have done if you had got into such a situation?' Moody replied, 'Man, I would never have got into it.' That's more than just common sense – that's wisdom!

O God, help me to help myself. Please show me how to avoid circumstances that make a fall almost inevitable. Amen.

Don't go on his ground

FOR READING AND MEDITATION
PROVERBS 4:10–27

'Let your eyes look straight ahead, fix your gaze directly before you.' (v.25)

We continue looking at the issue of keeping sex within marriage. Anatole France tells a story in which God and the devil are talking of a beautiful young girl. God asks, 'How dare you tempt such a lovely creature as that?' The devil replies, 'Well, she came on to my ground.' The best strategy with temptation is not to go near it. Paul's advice to Timothy was 'Flee from all this' (1 Tim. 6:11). John Ruskin says, 'No one can honestly ask to be delivered from temptation unless he has honestly and firmly determined to do the best he can to keep out of it.' My advice to every unmarried man and woman reading these lines – and married people, too – is this: Keep out of the devil's territory. Don't go on to his ground.

O God, make me alert to the dangers that beset my path, and if I do move towards them unsuspectingly, may warning bells ring in my heart. Amen.

Take it on faith!

FOR READING AND MEDITATION
PROVERBS 6:16–26

'My son, keep your father's commands and do not forsake your mother's teaching.' (v.20)

God doesn't give His prohibitions because sex is a bad thing; they are there to protect us from engaging in a good and beautiful thing in the wrong context. Within marriage, sexual activity is the doing of the right thing in the right place. Christians are, or should be, people who take God on trust. There's not much point in confessing to be a follower of Jesus Christ if you don't believe what He tells you in His Word and change it to suit your convenience. The concept of deferred satisfaction is a vital one for every young person to grasp, for without it there can be no real maturity. You must learn to deny yourself now so that in the future you may experience the right thing in the right way.

Father, take me by the hand lest I succumb to the temptation of immediate satisfaction. Please guide me and hold me. Amen.

Prepare!

FOR READING AND MEDITATION
PROVERBS 6:1–11

'Go to the ant, you sluggard; consider its ways and be wise!' (v.6)

The concept of deferred satisfaction and the wisdom of learning to wait whilst preparing for the future applies to everyone regardless of age. The harvester ant doesn't spend all its time eating. Instead it runs back and forth carrying food into the nest so that it may survive the winter when there will be no food. Learn from its example. Prepare for the future in every way you can. Deny yourself now the things that God puts out of bounds, but also give yourself to the things you need to know to improve your abilities in your chosen profession or vocation. Whatever you plan to do in the days ahead of you – prepare by study and also by prayer. Don't take His blessing for granted – *prepare*.

Father, forgive me for not giving myself to the tasks to which You have called me. Help me to be a prepared person. In Jesus' name I ask it. Amen.

Giving all to God

FOR READING AND MEDITATION
PROVERBS 8:1–11

'Choose my instruction instead of silver, knowledge rather than choice gold …' (v.10)

Consider this idea of deferred satisfaction by looking at sportsmen and women – especially in the Olympic Games. You see these contestants pushing themselves almost beyond endurance in order to gain a prize for themselves, their club or their country. Their rigorous training regime involves going through the pain barrier. The pressure, the denial of legitimate pleasures, the strong self-discipline, the tough training, are all outweighed by the hope of winning. If non-Christians can deny themselves present satisfaction for future gains and go to such lengths to win a prize, how much more ought we, who serve the risen Christ? Dare we stand by and watch them do for gold what we are not prepared to do for God? (1 Cor. 9:24–27.)

Father, help me to see the end from the beginning and to use all my powers in reaching for the goal. Amen.

Sin breaks God's heart

FOR READING AND MEDITATION
PROVERBS 6:27–35

'But a man who commits adultery lacks judgment;
whoever does so destroys himself.' (v.32)

Chastity is purity prior to marriage; faithfulness is purity in marriage. Love cannot be love unless it includes faithfulness. Marriage is a covenant and we often read in the Bible about the covenant aspect of love: 'He is a faithful God, keeping his covenant of love ...' (Deut. 7:9). God is depicted as a faithful husband to His faithless wife of Israel. God keeps His covenants even though they are broken by the other side. People may shy away from commitment in a relationship, claiming they want to be 'free' – but without commitment is it really love? Love is a commitment, and when men and women indulge in sex before marriage or a so-called affair they don't just break God's laws; they also break His heart.

O Father, in an age when anything goes, may I be an
exhibition to the world around of what it means to be a
follower of You. Help me to keep all my relationships pure.
For Your dear name's sake. Amen.

Be a person of passion

FOR READING AND MEDITATION
PROVERBS 29:1–18

'Where there is no revelation, the people cast off restraint …' (v.18)

What every one of us needs in our lives is a passion so powerful that it transcends all other passions. In God we find that passion. When our lives are touched by Him and we drink from His life-giving stream, our hearts are filled with a passion that keeps every other passion under control. Is not this what happened to Joseph? When Potiphar's wife tried to seduce him he fled from the house crying, 'How then could I do such a wicked thing and sin against God?' (Gen. 39:9). His passion for God overwhelmed all other passions. When Christ, who is the wisdom of God and the power of God, is allowed to live at the centre of our lives then His passion keeps every other passion where it ought to be – under control.

O Christ, come into my being afresh and light the fire of passion for You that will bring every other passion in my life under its complete control. Amen.

'Honeysuckle Christians'

FOR READING AND MEDITATION
PROVERBS 11:25–31

'A generous man will prosper; he who refreshes others will himself be refreshed.' (v.25)

I consider the fourth pillar of wisdom to be – *generosity*. We must not take today's text to mean that we ought to be generous because it brings its own rewards. Generosity that is exercised simply for the purpose of reward is not true generosity. I love the way in which Charles Harthern described giving: 'Some give like a sponge – only when they are squeezed. Some give like Moses' rock – only when they are hit. True Christians, however, give like the honeysuckle – because they delight to give.' That's the secret – giving because we delight to give. The generous hand comes from a generous heart. If the heart is not generous then, however much the hand gives, there is no true generosity.

Father, I ask for the blessing not only of trust, integrity and personal purity, but of generosity also. In Jesus' name I pray. Amen.

Divine mathematics

FOR READING AND MEDITATION
PROVERBS 11:16–24

'One man gives freely, yet gains even more; another withholds unduly, but comes to poverty.' (v.24)

Today's text is, of course, difficult for some to accept because it violates all the rules of mathematics. But God has a different set of mathematical rules. For example – what do five and two make? Seven? Yes, in man's arithmetic, but not in God's. In God's arithmetic five and two make five ... thousand. How come, I hear you say? Well, five loaves and two fish – the little lunch which a boy once gave to Jesus – were taken by Him and turned into enough food to feed five thousand (see John 6:1–13). And just to add to the point – 12 baskets of leftovers were gathered up by the disciples after everyone had eaten their fill! The more you give away the more you have, and the less you give the poorer you become.

O God, You who are always reaching out to me in generosity and love, help me this day to do the same. Amen.

'Giving with a warm hand'

FOR READING AND MEDITATION
PROVERBS 22:1–9

'A generous man will himself be blessed ...' (v.9)

You do not have to be rich in order to be generous. A pauper can give like a prince, providing he or she has the right spirit. An old Jewish saying puts it like this: 'The man who gives with a smile gives more than the man who gives with a frown.' It is the *spirit* of generosity that the Bible focuses on first of all – the spirit that gives, not because it wants to get something in return, but because it simply delights to give. One person has defined generosity as 'giving with a warm hand'. I like that. Who likes to receive anything from a cold hand? The opposite of generosity is selfishness, and just as generosity is a facet of wisdom so selfishness is a facet of foolishness.

O God, help me to be a person who gives 'with a warm hand'. Fire me with a passion to give. In Jesus' name I ask it. Amen.

The generous eye

FOR READING AND MEDITATION
PROVERBS 28:18–28

'He who gives to the poor will lack nothing ...' (v.27)

Jesus made a powerful statement, recorded in Matthew 6:22, which in the Moffatt translation reads: '... if your Eye is generous, the whole of your body will be illumined.' 'If your Eye ...' These words indicate that if your whole outlook on life, your whole way of looking at things, is generous then your whole personality is filled with light. Jesus was generous towards all – the poor, the outcasts of society, the sinful, the unlovely – and His whole personality was full of light. When we are in touch with Jesus, the fount of all wisdom, then He generates that same generosity within us. We begin to see everyone and everything with the same generous eye. Generosity, like love, never fails.

Lord Jesus, Your generous eye saw in me things I could never see in myself. May Your generosity generate generosity in me. Amen.

Suppose ... just suppose ...

FOR READING AND MEDITATION
PROVERBS 3:19–35

'Do not say to your neighbour, "Come back later; I'll give it tomorrow" – when you now have it with you.' (v.28)

Suppose, just suppose, the little boy who gave his loaves and fishes to Jesus (John 6:9) had said to himself, 'This meal is mine and I won't share it with anyone.' Suppose Ananias had not generously shared what God had given him with Saul who was to become the great missionary apostle (Acts 9:17). I have no doubt that today, and certainly in the immediate future, we will come across opportunities to be generous. If we fail to respond to these opportunities, who knows what rivers will never flow, what great ministries will never be initiated, what mighty things will not get done? God has opened His doors and been generous to us; let us not fail to open up our doors and be generous to others.

O Father, may I be the channel and not the stopping place of all Your generosity to me. Help me, dear Father. In Jesus' name. Amen.

A framework for generosity

FOR READING AND MEDITATION
PROVERBS 11:1–10

'The LORD abhors dishonest scales, but accurate weights are his delight.' (v.1)

How do we go about establishing a framework for generosity? Here are my suggestions. First, decide that nothing you possess is your own but that everything you have belongs to God. You are now ready to manage His possessions, not as you like but as He likes. Second, go over your life and see what can be classed as your needs and what merely constitutes your wants. Beyond your needs, what you have belongs to the needs of others. How do you decide what can be classed as your needs? Go over your life item by item and ask the Lord for directions, not forgetting the need of savings! Third, fix it as an axiom in your mind that you will be generous to people not to get a blessing but to be a blessing.

Father, I am thankful that my life is fixed in You and from that foundation I am able to build a framework for generosity. Help me to give freely and willingly. Amen.

Completing the framework

FOR READING AND MEDITATION
PROVERBS 14:27–35

'… whoever is kind to the needy honours God.' (v.31)

My fourth suggestion is this: give at least a tenth of your earnings to God's work. The giving of a tithe is seen by many as legalistic, but the tithe is really an acknowledgement that all that we have, including the remaining nine-tenths, belongs to God. Fifth, make your will under God's direction and maintain a balance between responsibility for your family and the continuing work of God. Sixth, remember that the principle of generosity applies not only to your treasure but also to your talents and your time. Seventh, accept the smallest opportunity to be generous as a training ground for faithfulness. Why does the Bible make so much of generosity? Because the truly generous are the truly wise.

Father, like Simon Peter, who gave Your Son his boat from which to preach, I give You my treasure, my talents and my time for You to use as Your pulpit. Amen.

'A disturbing of complacency'

FOR READING AND MEDITATION
PROVERBS 13:1–10

'The sluggard craves and gets nothing, but the desires of the diligent are fully satisfied.' (v.4)

I believe the fifth of the seven pillars of wisdom is – *diligence*. The wise persevere, persist in following that which is right, stick with it and never give up. I used to be complacent and lacked application but a year or so after my conversion an uncle of mine said to my father, 'I wondered whether he had been really converted but by his diligence I can see he has found God.' Forgive the personal emphasis, but if it had not been for the diligence I learned at the feet of Christ I would not have been able to write *Every Day with Jesus* for over 40 years. I learned diligence from the One whose life and character were the very epitome of this quality – Jesus. He is diligence personified.

Father, I long for diligence. Prune from me all inertia and indolence, all lethargy and dodging of responsibility, all complacency and pride. Amen.

'A second wind'

FOR READING AND MEDITATION
PROVERBS 10:1-8

'Lazy hands make a man poor, but diligent hands bring wealth.' (v.4)

Yesterday we said, 'Jesus is diligence personified'. The purpose for which Jesus came into the world inwardly pressed Him forward, despite the threats and obstacles that came His way, and He pursued the task right to the end. A middle-aged lady I knew who found the Lord said, 'Christ gave me a second wind in the race of life.' I wonder, as you read these notes, are you on the point of giving up a task in which you know you are rightly engaged? Have lethargy, inertia and indifference crept in and threatened to take over your soul? Reach up and put your hand in the hand of Jesus. Talk with Him now and draw from Him the strength you need. Then in His name go out and throw yourself once again into the task.

Loving Father, help me to be diligent and use that special grace to Your praise and glory. Amen.

Know the difference

FOR READING AND MEDITATION
PROVERBS 4:10–27

'Above all else, guard your heart, for it is the wellspring of life.' (v.23)

When contrasting diligence and obstinacy, a student wrote, 'One is a strong will and the other is a strong won't.' Diligence is dogged perseverance; obstinacy is dogged inflexibility and self-will. When Jesus came to Calvary, He said, 'I have finished the work which You [the Father] have given Me to do' (John 17:4, NKJV). Notice the word 'You'. There were many who would have liked Jesus to do this and that, to go here and go there, but He did only what the Father required Him to do. Saying 'yes' to God's will and pursuing it is diligence. Saying 'yes' to a thing that is not God's will and pursuing that is obstinacy. We had better learn the difference or we will live in perpetual disillusionment.

Father, help me differentiate between diligence and obstinacy so that I can finish the work which You have given me to do. Amen.

The secret of survival

FOR READING AND MEDITATION
PROVERBS 12:11–28

'Diligent hands will rule, but laziness ends in slave labour.' (v.24)

Victor Frankl, a Jew, was an Austrian neurologist and psychiatrist who survived the Holocaust and the horror of the concentration camps. He discovered that those who had a meaning or purpose to live for, such as the hope of seeing a loved one again, found it easier to keep going despite the greatest odds, while those who had no meaning or purpose simply gave up. Frankl discovered by empirical means what another Jew discovered by revelation – that in order to persist, we need hope. That other Jew was the apostle Paul, and he showed even greater understanding than Frankl when he said, 'Christ in you, the hope of glory' (Col. 1:27). Christ *with* us is one thing; Christ *in* us – now that's another.

O Father, Christ's presence within gives me a hope that provides meaning in the deepest and darkest moments of my life. Amen.

Life is a task

FOR READING AND MEDITATION
PROVERBS 2:1–11

'… applying your heart to understanding … then you will … find the knowledge of God.' (vv.2,5)

Frankl said that the reason so many people are unhappy is because they fail to understand that life is not just something to be enjoyed but rather it is a task. So near yet so far! Yes, in many ways life is a task, a tough one that is sometimes almost unbearable. That's why we need to have Jesus at the centre of our lives. We then pursue the divine task with the help of divine grace. Both the writer of Proverbs and Victor Frankl said that life works better when we give ourselves to it with diligence, but there is much more to it than this. Why do you think God inspired the writer of Proverbs to personify wisdom? Because, as we saw, it prepares us to face the fact that true wisdom is not merely found in principles but in a Person. And that Person is Jesus Christ.

Thank You Father, that through Jesus I dwell in wisdom and am indwelt by it. You give me divine strength for the divine task. Amen.

What's the point?

FOR READING AND MEDITATION
PROVERBS 21:1–15

'The plans of the diligent lead to profit as surely as haste leads to poverty.' (v.5)

What is the point of diligence? Why keep persevering with a task? I'll tell you why. It is because it is in the arena of perseverance that true character is forged, shaped, tempered and polished. It is in the daily grind – in the hard and often tedious duties of life – that the character of Jesus is given the maximum opportunity to be reproduced in us, replacing what Charles Swindoll calls that 'thin, fragile internal theology with a tough reliable set of convictions that enable us to handle life rather than escape from it'. Paul rejoiced in suffering for it produces perseverance, character and hope (Rom. 5:3–4). Without diligence, we will stumble and fall. With it, we can survive and overcome.

O God, help me see that out of the raw materials of human living I must fashion the important quality of diligence. In Jesus' name. Amen.

The Four Spiritual Flaws

FOR READING AND MEDITATION
PROVERBS 20:1–13

'A sluggard does not plough in season; so at harvest time he looks but finds nothing.' (v.4)

The 'Four Spiritual Flaws' are four common misconceptions concerning the tough questions and difficult tasks of the Christian life, and unless they are nailed, diligence will have no meaning. *Flaw No. 1*: Once you become a Christian, you will never have any more problems. *Flaw No. 2*: If you are having problems then you must be lacking in some way spiritually. *Flaw No. 3*: Never admit to anything being a problem; if you do, negativism will take over your life. *Flaw No. 4*: All problems and questions can be resolved by the application of the right verses of Scripture. None of these are true. What is true, however, is that Christ will be there to share our problems and get us through them. Diligence must keep us going.

Father, I would be rid of all flawed thinking. Show me that I am not called to understand, but to stand. Give me grace to keep going even in the face of unanswered questions. In Jesus' name I pray. Amen.

Diligence does pay off

FOR READING AND MEDITATION
PROVERBS 24:23–34

'Thorns had come up everywhere, the ground was covered with weeds ...' (v.31)

What are diligence and perseverance all about? They involve sticking to a task you know God wants you to do until it is completed, despite difficulties and frustrations. Diligence does pay off. Have you heard the story of the two frogs who fell into a bucket of cream? They tried very hard to get out by climbing up the side of the bucket, but each time they slipped back again. Finally, one said, 'We'll never get out of here,' so he gave up, stopped kicking and drowned. The other frog persevered and kicked and kicked and kicked. Suddenly, he felt something hard beneath his feet and discovered that his kicking had turned the cream into butter. He hopped on top of it and was able to leap out to safety.

Father, give me, I pray, this aspect of wisdom so that, like a postage stamp, I will stick to one thing until I get there. In Jesus' name I ask it. Amen.

The weight of words

FOR READING AND MEDITATION
PROVERBS 10:9–17

*'The mouth of the righteous is a fountain of life, but
violence overwhelms the mouth of the wicked.' (v.11)*

The sixth pillar of wisdom is: *watchfulness with words.*
Anyone who fails to understand the importance of
words and the effect they can have for good or bad is
not a wise person. Today's text implies that there is a
transfer of wisdom from one person to another when
wise words are used, but that unwise words have the
opposite effect. I often talk to couples about the power
of their words. Words have the potential to destroy or
build up, to hurt or heal, to bless or blister, to bring
comfort or consternation. Life-long emotional scars
can be left by bitter words. With words, God created
a world. We do the same. Our words create a world of
order or disorder, of cosmos or chaos. Be wise – watch
your words.

*Father, give me the wisdom to use words in a way that will
build up and not pull down, construct and not destruct.
Amen.*

Words that scar

FOR READING AND MEDITATION
PROVERBS 12:11–28

'Reckless words pierce like a sword, but the tongue of the wise brings healing.' (v.18)

Have you ever used these words in the school playground: 'Sticks and stones may break my bones, but words will never hurt me'? It's not true. Unkind or cutting words are like deadly missiles that penetrate all the soul's defences and blast a hole in the personality, creating damage that may take years to repair. On the other hand, words that are encouraging can lift and cheer the soul in a way that is quite amazing. How wonderful it will be if today you and I can say a cheerful and encouraging word to someone that will bless them, lighten their darkness, and minister the life of God into their soul. At least let's try! May we, like Barnabas be sons and daughters of encouragement (Acts 4:36).

O Father, having looked into the mirror of Your Word I see what I should be. Please help me to be that person. In Jesus' name. Amen.

Driven personalities

FOR READING AND MEDITATION
PROVERBS 18:1–24

'The tongue has the power of life and death ...' (v.21)

Every time a father lost his temper he told his son, 'You are not going to amount to anything.' Thirty years later the man still bore the pain of his father's verbal malpractice and was *driven* to prove his father wrong. This man was *driven* by the lash of bitter and cruel words spoken to him years earlier. Take, on the other hand, this example of another man to whom I talked some time ago. He told me that his father used to hug him every day and say, 'You are so special to me. There is no one in this world who could take your place.' That man grew up full of life and with a personality characterised by optimism. Proverbs is right: death words destroy, life words build up and give increasing strength.

Father, I would be a builder and not a destroyer of human personalities. Help me keep a check on my speech and use words as You would use them. Amen.

Healing words

FOR READING AND MEDITATION
PROVERBS 15:1–15

'The tongue that brings healing is a tree of life ...' (v.4)

When Sigmund Freud found that symptoms of emotional distress could be relieved simply by talking in certain ways to his patients, he was deeply interested and intrigued. If Freud had spent some time reading the book of Proverbs he might have been less surprised. His training in 'the medical model' had conditioned him to think of people as merely biological and chemical entities whose problems arose from physical malfunctioning. When people put their feelings into words it seems as if the pent-up emotion flows out through the words. Now, most effective psychotherapy has to do with letting people talk and verbally encouraging them. Thank God that life, as well as death, lies in the power of the tongue.

Father, help me minister life through my tongue this very day. Give me opportunities to put into action what I have learned. Amen.

The most powerful word

FOR READING AND MEDITATION
PROVERBS 25:11–28

'As a north wind brings rain, so a sly tongue brings angry looks.' (v.23)

Someone has compiled a list of the most powerful words in the English language: 'The bitterest word – alone. The most revered word – mother. The most feared word – death. The coldest word – no. The warmest word – friend.' What, I wonder, is the most powerful word you have ever come across? I will tell you mine – Jesus. Charles Colson tells of visiting a man on death row. The man had been in a foetal position for months and would not speak. Charles told him the gospel and asked him to say the name Jesus. A week later the man was sitting in his chair, shaven, and the cell swept clean. He said, 'Jesus lives here now.' He went to the electric chair but his last words were: 'I'm going to be with the Lord.'

O Father, when I utter the name Jesus something profound happens within me. May I learn and appropriate all the power that lies behind that name. Amen.

A disciplined tongue

FOR READING AND MEDITATION
PROVERBS 10:18–32

'… he who holds his tongue is wise.' (v.19)

It's important to talk, but talking too much can be as bad as not talking at all. Proverbs extols rationing our words. Once, when writing a prescription, a doctor asked a woman to put out her tongue. When he had finished she said, 'But, doctor, you never even looked at my tongue.' The doctor replied, 'It wasn't necessary, I just wanted you to keep quiet while I wrote the prescription.' A wise person is someone who has a disciplined tongue. Many need to learn this for, just like the tongue in old lace-up shoes, our tongue is often the last thing to be worn out. If that is true of you ask for God's help, for an undisciplined tongue is an unloving tongue.

Father, I realise that often my tongue is the most difficult thing to bring under control. I give you my tongue to be bridled – please take over the reins. Amen.

We become what we say

FOR READING AND MEDITATION
PROVERBS 21:16-31

'He who guards his mouth and his tongue keeps himself from calamity.' (v.23)

Why is this self-discipline of the tongue so important? It is because the expression of a thing deepens the impression. A word uttered becomes a word made flesh – in us. We become the incarnation of what we express. If you tell a lie, you become a lie. You have to live with someone you cannot trust. A brilliant young physicist says that he often discusses complex issues relating to physics with his wife, who doesn't know the first thing about the subject. He told a friend, 'I describe in detail what I am doing and she doesn't understand a word. But sometimes when I'm through – *I do*.' When we express good things, positive things, loving things, scriptural things, these things go deeper into us.

O Father, cleanse me deep within so that I may be pure in soul as well as speech, and honour You in all I do. Amen.

The cause of most friction

FOR READING AND MEDITATION
PROVERBS 16:21–33

'Pleasant words are a honeycomb, sweet to the soul and healing to the bones.' (v.24)

I am convinced that most of the friction in human relationships is caused not so much by the words we speak as by the tone of voice in which we speak them. What we say is important, of course, but how we say it is also important. Our speech conveys our thoughts; our tone of voice, however, conveys our mood. How easy it is to say, 'I love you', in a tone that conveys the very opposite. What is our conclusion after considering the subject of words? Is it not this: the wise are those who understand how their words can impact another person, for good or for bad, and commit themselves to using words only as Paul instructs us in Ephesians 4:29 – words that are 'helpful for building others up'.

O God, I ask once more that You will help me to hold my tongue when I should and to speak when I should using the right tone. Amen.

'A single soul in two bodies'

FOR READING AND MEDITATION
PROVERBS 22:10–16

'He who loves a pure heart and whose speech is gracious will have the king for his friend.' (v.11)

The final pillar of wisdom is that of *friendship*. The wise are those who know how to make friends and remain loyal to them. What exactly is friendship? A Christian magazine offered a prize for the best definition of friendship sent in by its readers. Hundreds of definitions were received and the one that was given first prize was this: 'A friend is the one who comes in when the whole world has gone out.' My own definition of friendship is this: 'Friendship is the knitting of one soul with another so that both become stronger and better by virtue of their relationship.' I like also the definition of an ancient philosopher who said that friendship was 'a single soul dwelling in two bodies'.

Father, teach me the art of making friends. Help me see at the very beginning that being a friend is more important than having a friend. Amen.

The fusion of friendship

FOR READING AND MEDITATION
ECCLESIASTES 4:1–12

'Though one may be overpowered, two can defend themselves. A cord of three strands is not quickly broken.'
(v.12)

Why is friendship so important? The point being made in today's verse is this: when you are in a close relationship with another person you not only have what the other person gives to you in the friendship, or you to the other person, but you have a third quality – a strength and a power which comes out of the relationship and which you could never have known had you both stayed apart. In other words, in the fusion of friendship you discover a power that could never be discovered were you not bound together in the relationship of friendship. Your strength plus your friend's strength produces a new and even greater strength.

Father, now I see into the heart and meaning of friendship. Out of it comes a power and strength that is greater than the sum of the two parts. Amen.

Synergy

FOR READING AND MEDITATION
PROVERBS 17:1–17

'A friend loves at all times, and a brother is born for adversity.' (v.17)

In friendship there is a new energy that was never there before. The word that is often used to describe this is 'synergy', which the dictionary defines as 'the combined effect of two things that exceeds the sum of their individual effects'. It simply means that the whole is greater than the sum of its two parts. When you put two pieces of wood together in a certain way they hold much more than the total of the weight held by each separately. One plus one equals three or more. A friendship can be exhilarating, exciting, and at times exhausting. But it can also open up new possibilities, new trails, new adventures, new territories and new continents. We live deprived lives if we live without friends.

Father, I see that I am made for relationships, not isolation. Help me understand this principle of synergy and see it at work with my friends. Amen.

'A friend with skin on'

FOR READING AND MEDITATION
PROVERBS 27:17–27

'As iron sharpens iron, so one man sharpens another.' (v.17)

I have heard some Christians say, 'Why do I need friends? God is my Friend – isn't that enough?' Such questions demonstrate a lack of understanding of the purpose of human relationships. Yes, God is our Friend, but we need human friends also. 'To be,' said someone, 'is to be in relationships.' You won't know who you are or become fully mature until you are in a relationship. This might be difficult for some to accept, but the more effectively we relate on a horizontal level with our human friends, the more effectively we will relate on a vertical level with our heavenly Friend. Yes, God is our Friend – our closest Friend – but, as a little boy once put it, 'We need friends with skin on also.'

Father, I see that my best friend brings out the best in me. Help me to be a best friend to someone – and to bring out the best in that person. Amen.

Steps to friendship

FOR READING AND MEDITATION
PROVERBS 18:1–24

'A man of many companions may come to ruin, but there is a friend who sticks closer than a brother.' (v.24)

How do we go about making friends? The first step is *be friendly*. 'A man who has friends must himself be friendly' (Prov. 18:24, NKJV). Dale Carnegie said, 'You can make more friends in two months by becoming interested in other people than you can in two years by trying to get other people interested in you.' The main reason why some people have no friends is because they demonstrate an unfriendly attitude. To have a friend – be one. The second step is *allow time for friendships to develop*. In friendship it is futile to try to force doors open. Instead, be like Christ in the book of Revelation (Rev. 3:20); stand reverently at the door – and knock. Only if the door is opened from within should you go ahead.

Father, show me not only how to sympathise with my friends' weaknesses, but how to draw out their strength. In Jesus' name. Amen.

When not a true friend

FOR READING AND MEDITATION
PROVERBS 27:1–9

'Wounds from a friend can be trusted ...' (v.6)

The third step in order to win friends is *be prepared to be vulnerable*. By this I mean be prepared to be hurt. No relationship is free from pain this side of eternity – so don't expect perfection in your friendships. Fourth, *love your friend enough to talk with him or her about anything you feel is not right*. One of the greatest tests of friendship is to ask yourself: Am I prepared to lose this friendship in the interests of God's kingdom? If not, then you haven't got a true friendship. Fifth, *allow your friend to have other friends also*. Don't suffocate your friend by being possessive and demanding that he or she maintain just your friendship and no one else's.

O Father, help me to be vulnerable to others and may I never suffocate a friendship by being possessive. In Jesus' name I pray. Amen.

No one has a double

FOR READING AND MEDITATION
PROVERBS 27:10–16

'Do not forsake your friend ...' (v.10)

The sixth and final step to developing friendship: *stay loyal and loving to your friends as far as you possibly can.* God made us for relationships and it is His will that we cultivate a circle of friends. Every friend is different. No one has a double in friendship. The more we have, the richer we are. Dr Lawrence Crabb says, 'Every day we ought to move out from our base in the home and say to ourselves: Lord, help me reach out and touch someone deep in their being today, not for the rewards it brings me in terms of good feelings, but for the blessing I can be to them.' This is the way in which Jesus lived and related to others. Perhaps this is why they called Him 'a *friend* of ... "sinners"' (Matt. 11:19).

Father, guide me in my future days so that in every relationship I may be able to apply the principles I have just learned. In Jesus' name I ask it. Amen.

Growing in wisdom

FOR READING AND MEDITATION
PROVERBS 9:10–18

'The fear of the LORD is the beginning of wisdom, and knowledge of the Holy One is understanding.' (v.10)

My prayer is that these meditations will stimulate thousands to pursue that most glorious of all qualities – divine wisdom. But remember, do not seek wisdom for its own sake. Seek it so that you might more effectively represent Jesus Christ. And beware of legalism, that soul-destroying attitude that takes greater pleasure in principles than in the Person who is behind them – our Lord Jesus Christ Himself. If you still don't know Him then bow your head this very moment, repent of every sin you have committed and quietly surrender your heart and life into His hands. Committing your way to God is the beginning of wisdom; continual trust in Him will see it develop and grow.

Father, please grant me this wisdom, that I might know You better, love You more, and do Your perfect will. Amen.

'Nothing missed'

FOR READING AND MEDITATION
JEREMIAH 29:1–14

'"For I know the plans I have for you," declares the LORD ...'
(v.11)

O ne of the most exciting ideas I have come across in my journey through the Christian life is the thought that in every believer's life a divine story is being written. Through all the countless occurrences of our lives a guiding hand is at work, taking the raw material of life and making from it a story-line that, even though it may be hidden from us at the moment, will, when viewed from the vantage point of eternity, astonish us. Everything in our story has a point. Nothing need be irrelevant. This is the thought that must grip us as we begin our meditations over these next two months: behind the seemingly chaotic and indiscriminate events of our lives a bigger story, a *divine* story, is being written.

O Father, everything that happens to me is being used to form a story. You turn everything into something meaningful. And I am so grateful. Amen.

More than just facts

FOR READING AND MEDITATION
COLOSSIANS 3:1–17

'For you died, and your life is now hidden with Christ in God.' (v.3)

We must learn to see our lives as far more than a compilation of facts, otherwise we are in danger of regarding a person merely as a biological machine. Even in the seemingly most humdrum life a story is being created that, seen from an eternal perspective, would be breathtaking. You may think your life is boring and routine, but if you are a Christian then the sovereign God is at work, weaving every fact into a story. Don't get caught up, I beg you, with the world's ideas to such an extent that you forget, as our text for today puts it, that 'your life is now hidden with Christ in God'. Any life that is in Christ has a meaning that extends far beyond what is obvious from the happenings down here on earth.

O Father, how can I ever thank You enough for the fact that my life is hidden with Christ in You? Help me be fully aware of its wonder. Amen.

The elements of story

FOR READING AND MEDITATION
I THESSALONIANS 5:12–28

'And we urge you ... be patient with everyone.' (v.14)

I was once told a story should have four elements: (1) characters; (2) a plot; (3) movement; (4) dénouement. A good story has many different *characters* and in your story and mine there is a variety of characters: friends, enemies, people who are for us and people who are against us. The people in your life, I believe, are hand-picked by the Lord to expose your temper, pride, stubbornness – whatever your struggles and difficulties might be. And running away from them is no answer. It's not worth it because God has many more such people to replace them. God wants to make us like Jesus, and one of the ways He goes about this is by using the people who cross our paths as tools to shape us and make us more like Christ.

O Father, help me grasp the fact that relationships do not so much cause problems as reveal problems. Grant that I may not miss the lessons You are trying to teach me. Amen.

The divine plot

FOR READING AND MEDITATION
ROMANS 8:28–39

*'For those God foreknew he also predestined to be
conformed to the likeness of his Son ...' (v.29)*

Today we look at the second element of story: *plot*. The
dictionary defines 'plot' as a 'plan of main events or
topics in a play, poem, novel etc'. God, as we have been
saying, is in the story-telling business too. But what is
His plot? John Stott expresses it like this: 'God is making
human beings more human by making them more like
Christ.' God is so excited about His Son Jesus Christ that
He wants to make everyone like Him, not in appearance,
of course, but in character. And He uses everything that
happens to us – good, bad and indifferent – to make us
more like Him. What a difference it would make if we
would really get hold of the truth that God allows into
our lives only what He can use.

*Father, help me grasp the fact that You allow into my life
only those things that fulfil your purpose and help me to
become more like Jesus. Amen.*

'I'll wait until I get home'

FOR READING AND MEDITATION
I CORINTHIANS 13:1–13

'... when perfection comes, the imperfect disappears.' (v.10)

The third aspect of good story-telling is: *movement*. This has to do with the way a story unfolds. Eugene Peterson defines Christian counselling as 'listening to someone's story and looking for the movement of God'. He assumes that God is always actively doing something in a Christian's life, even in times of trouble. Certain dark problems have occurred in my own life that I have never been able fully to understand. *Some* light shines upon those problems, but no *complete* solution is to hand. However, enough light beats on our path for us to pick our way along it. But for the final explanation we must wait until we get home, and then our heavenly Father will explain it to us Himself.

Father help me in those moments when I can find no answers to trust You even when I cannot trace You. In Christ's name I ask it. Amen.

All's well that ends well

FOR READING AND MEDITATION
2 CORINTHIANS 4:1–18

'For our light and momentary troubles are achieving for us an eternal glory that far outweighs them all.' (v.17)

The fourth aspect of good story-telling is *dénouement* – the final resolution. How will the story of my own life end? What special skill will the Divine Author apply to the final details of my personal narrative? As I mused, I remembered something that C.S. Lewis said, which came home to me with great force, that it is as if we ride with our backs to the engine ... we have no notion of what stage of the journey we have reached; that we can only understand a story when we have heard it all. G.K. Chesterton said that you cannot finish a sum how you like, but you can finish a story how you like. All of God's stories end well. I trust Him to do this. And so, my friend, must you.

Loving heavenly Father, may I so live that nothing I do will hinder You writing the conclusion You have planned for my story. Amen.

God at work

FOR READING AND MEDITATION
PHILIPPIANS 2:1–18

'... it is God who works in you to will and to act according to his good purpose.' (v.13)

We continue reflecting on the fact that in every believer's life a divine story is being written. We simply have to believe this. Because God is at work in our lives, we can be assured that a wonderful story is being written, in which all the puzzling parts will finally fit – everything will eventually come together. There is a beautiful park and boating lake in Scarborough, Yorkshire, called The Mere. Not many who are impressed with its charm know that it was created out of a garbage heap. Originally it was one of Scarborough's refuse dumps, but with scientific thoroughness and the strictest regard for hygiene the city fathers transformed it into a thing of beauty. And if man can do that, what of God?

Gracious Father, how can I thank You enough that Your transforming power is constantly at work in my life? Blessed be Your name for ever. Amen.

An unfolding creation

FOR READING AND MEDITATION
MATTHEW 18:1–9

'If your hand or your foot causes you to sin, cut if off and throw it away.' (v.8)

J.R.R. Tolkien said that a Christian could actually assist in the unfolding and enrichment of creation in their own responses to events. In C.S. Lewis's *The Silver Chair* the beautiful Queen of the Underworld nearly convinces the children from the Overworld that her own dismal kingdom is the only reality, and theirs but an imagined dream. However, the Marsh-wiggle, to prevent the Queen's words taking hold, thrusts his foot into the fire. The shock helps him face reality, and as he speaks up, the children see the point he is making, run to his side, and escape. Can you think of anything that more imaginatively builds on the words of our Lord that we have read in today's text?

O Father, may my responses to events enrich the story of my life and prove a godly example to others. In Jesus' name. Amen.

Is this idea biblical?

FOR READING AND MEDITATION
PSALM 94:1–23

'Does he who implanted the ear not hear? Does he who formed the eye not see?' (v.9)

What biblical foundation is there for believing that God is a story writer? Several verses suggest God is the Author of our story. One is Ephesians 2:10: 'For we are God's workmanship.' This text could also be translated 'We are God's *poem*.' Another is 2 Corinthians 3:3: 'You show that you are a letter from Christ.' If we combine these two texts we see that a Christian is to be God's poetry and God's prose. Our lives are to enshrine a divine mystery – poetry – and at the same time express a divine message – prose. Also, consider today's verse: if we find excitement in an imaginative and thrilling novel then what can we expect to find in real life when the Author is none other than the Almighty God?

Father, help me to see my life as a story that is scripted by the world's most innovative and inventive story writer. In Jesus' name. Amen.

Always ahead

FOR READING AND MEDITATION
MARK 16:1–8

'He has risen! … He is going ahead of you into Galilee.'
(vv.6–7)

When I realised that in every believer's life a divine story is being written, it changed my whole approach as a pastor and a counsellor. I saw that whenever I sat down with someone to listen to their personal problems, *the risen Christ had gone there ahead of me.* He was in that person's life, doing something, saying something, that with the Spirit's help I needed to understand. I realised that my task was much more than to perform the traditional pastoral role, read a few comforting texts and pray; I needed to be alert to the story God was writing in that person's life. My task then was to help them interpret that story and understand how to play their role in the bigger divine story that was unfolding.

O Lord, show me even more clearly that no matter what happens to me, You are always ahead. Amen.

'Prevenient grace'

FOR READING AND MEDITATION
PSALM 139:1–6

'You hem me in – behind and before; you have laid your hand upon me.' (v.5)

I happened to speak about the thought that the Master has gone ahead when I was attending a pastors' conference in Singapore. Afterwards a Chinese pastor said to me, 'From now on I will see my hospital visits and counselling sessions in a new light. Whenever I walk into a counselling room or a hospital ward I shall say to myself, "Christ has risen and is going before you."' And then he added, 'I am so intrigued with the idea that the Master is always ahead of me, that when I meet up with His children I am coming in on something that is already in progress. It has revolutionised my ministry.' Theologians call this 'prevenient grace'. Grace is *there* – even before we need it.

O Father, how wonderful it is to realise that Your grace is prevenient – that it is there even before I need it. Amen.

Paul's thorn in the flesh

FOR READING AND MEDITATION
2 CORINTHIANS 12:1–10

'Three times I pleaded with the Lord to take it away from me.' (v.8)

F ollowing on from what I said yesterday, I predict that unless Christian counsellors start to recognise that everyone's life is a story, unless they learn to listen to the story that God is telling in a person's life and go along with it, then they will fail to help people in the way they need to be helped. I suggested to one trainee that Christian counselling must have a much higher goal than that of solving problems; the goal must be *to know God in the problem*. If a counsellor's goal was the removal of Paul's problem he would have been working against the purposes of God. Clearly, the Lord was allowing the problem to continue because it served to make Paul a person more dependent upon the strength and power that only God could provide.

Father, thank You for reminding me that knowing You is the highest goal and not the solution of problems. Amen.

'The character on page 29'

FOR READING AND MEDITATION
EPHESIANS 1:11–23

' ... *according to the plan of him who works out everything in conformity with the purpose of his will ...' (v.11)*

A character in a novel might be in confusion and distress on page 29 but the author has already planned the way out later in their story. Maybe at the moment you are feeling confused and distressed but *you are only on page 29*. Take heart: up ahead the Divine Author is going to show you the significance of what is happening to you. Remember, He 'works out everything in conformity with the purpose of his will'. The important thing now is that you trust the Author and play your part well. That may involve helping another person, not letting others down, doing the loving thing even though you don't feel like it. You are part of a story – a much bigger story – and what you do counts – infinitely.

O Father, remind me, I pray, that things are working according to plan – to Your plans, not my plans. In Jesus' name I ask it. Amen.

'Tell me a story'

FOR READING AND MEDITATION
MARK 4:21–34

'He did not say anything to them without using a parable.' (v.34)

Both children and adults love to be told a story. Jesus used many stories because He knew how expert men and women are at arming themselves against the entrance of truth. And human nature doesn't change. Many of us, when we go to church, listen to the sermon that is preached from behind a mental barricade. We are on our guard lest something challenging gets past our defences and touches our conscience. But we listen to stories differently. A story glides unhindered into the very citadel of our mind, and the truth it conveys gains access before we guess its purpose. The story touches our conscience until it stings in confirmation of the point. The flag of surrender goes up and our soul capitulates.

Father, I see that You have given us an appetite for a story. May I understand how to use stories in my ministry to others. Amen.

Saved – by a story

FOR READING AND MEDITATION
2 SAMUEL 12:1–14

'Then David said to Nathan, "I have sinned against the Lord."' (v.13)

J.R.R. Tolkien said that man is a story-telling animal and for this reason God has given him a story to live. God saved David through a story after he had committed adultery with Bathsheba. It was probably the only way he could have been saved. God sent the prophet Nathan to him with a simple story about a rich man who had large flocks but who stole from a poor man his one little lamb and killed it. David was moved by the story, but because he had deceived himself so completely he could not see in it any application to himself. The next moment the prophet challenged him with these words: 'You are the man!' (v.7). The lie was exposed. The sophistry was at an end. David had been found out – by a story.

Father, I pray that I might see the application to myself in the truths, principles and stories You have recorded for my benefit in Scripture. Amen.

The most appealing stories

FOR READING AND MEDITATION
JOSHUA 24:1–18

' ... *choose for yourselves this day whom you will serve ...*'
(v.15)

The most appealing stories are those which contain elements of romance, adventure, heroism and important decisions. In fact, many sections of the Bible would lose something if these elements were absent. The story before us today is just one of the many Bible passages that show us that out of all the choices we are called upon to make in life, the most important one is to come over onto the Lord's side. But we certainly need to keep in mind that Bible stories, though full of romance and adventure, are not fairy tales but fact. These life-and-death issues are crucial. We must never forget this awesome truth: 'Man is destined to die once, and after that to face judgment' (Heb. 9:27).

Help me, Father, to read the Bible not as a page torn from the past but as a mirror that reflects where I am in my own personal journey of faith. Amen.

The process of being known

FOR READING AND MEDITATION
PSALM 32:1–11

'I will instruct you and teach you in the way you should go ...' (v.8)

One reason some Christians find it difficult to accept the concept of story has to do with feelings of self-rejection because they never felt accepted by those who nurtured them. They cannot believe that any human being could take an interest in them, let alone God. C.S. Lewis defines prayer as taking part in the process of being deeply known. God knows everything there is to know about an elephant, but the elephant cannot join in the process of being known. Only a person made in the image of God can do that. There are some who cannot joyfully join in the process of being known because they are convinced that if they were deeply known, they would be rejected.

O Father, what a thrilling thought that through prayer I can join in the process of being known. Thank You my Father. Amen.

God is interested

FOR READING AND MEDITATION
PSALM 139:7–24

'How precious to me are your thoughts, O God!' (v.17)

Another reason why some Christians doubt that their lives are part of a bigger story is this: they are not sure that God takes an interest in what happens to little them in the vastness of the cosmos. However, we hold to God's personal care and interest in our lives not *in spite* of God's greatness but *because* of it. Even though whirring worlds move at His word, He says to us, 'Be still, and *know* that I am God' (Psa. 46:10). He does not delegate the responsibility of developing the story-line of our lives to others. He does this Himself. Let this amazing thought sink into your consciousness today: the God before whom angels veil their faces condescends to involve Himself in the tiniest details of your life.

O God, the thought that You have a personal interest in all the details of my life is more than I can take in. Yet I must believe it for it is true. Amen.

Knowing God

FOR READING AND MEDITATION
PHILIPPIANS 3:1–11

'I want to know Christ and the power of his resurrection ...'
(v.10)

A third reason why some people find it difficult to believe that God is sufficiently interested in them to compose a story in their lives: they do not know Him well enough. How do we get to know Him? By spending time with Him in prayer and the study of His Word. It is difficult to arrange to see the Queen or spend time with her but easy to have an audience with the King of kings. All may come regardless of wealth, age, nationality, clothing, social standing or achievements. Of course, discipline is essential. It amazes me that people happily set aside several hours to master some hobby yet blandly suppose they can get to know God during a few sleepy moments at the end of the day.

O Father, how I long to know You better. Yet there is a cost in terms of discipline and time. Help me pay the price. In Jesus' name. Amen.

The Bible – a story

FOR READING AND MEDITATION
EPHESIANS 1:1–10

'... the mystery of his will ... to bring all things in heaven
and on earth together under ... Christ.' (vv.9–10)

The Bible is much more than prescriptions on how to
stop worrying, how to avoid anger, and so on. First
and foremost the Bible is a story – a story of how God
is at work, moving from a plan laid down in eternity to
a climax within history, and then on beyond time to the
future. The story that God is telling in each of our lives is
wonderful, but more wonderful still is the story that God
tells in the Scriptures. Over the years, in my own walk
with God, I have found a strange thing: the more I get
caught up in the story God is telling in the Bible, the less
preoccupied I become with my own personal problems. I
can assure you that nothing empowers daily living more
than being caught up in *His* story.

*O Father, open my eyes to see the big picture which the Bible
unfolds. Lead me on, dear Father. In Jesus' name. Amen.*

The illusion of depth

FOR READING AND MEDITATION
JOHN 10:1–21

'I am the gate; whoever enters through me will be saved.'
(v.9)

The disciplines of psychology and sociology have their place in the scheme of things, but they lack depth because they only focus on people themselves and exclude their role in the story of the kingdom of God. They are like a hall of mirrors, where you see different reflections of yourself. But that is all you see. Eventually you tire of seeing yourself and want to get out, you want to find the door. Jesus talked of Himself as the door or the gate, as we see from today's text. If you are looking for a new world – a world with depth – you will have to find the door. That door is Christ. And going through that door brings you to a much more exciting world than you could ever have imagined.

O Father, how glad I am that I have found that door. Through Your Son I enter a world that surpasses my greatest imagination. Amen.

God's wonderful storybook

FOR READING AND MEDITATION
GENESIS 24:1–67

'So they ... asked her, "Will you go with this man?"
"I will go," she said.' (v.58)

G.K. Chesterton said that God is the world's best story-teller. The stories in Scripture prepare us for great truths. Today's story gives us an insight into the wonderful way in which God sent His Holy Spirit into the world to seek out a Bride for His Son. Just as the servant in the story moved under the guidance of God until he at last found the one whom God had elected to be Isaac's wife, so the Spirit has moved (and is moving) through the world, seeking God's elected ones and preparing them for the day when the Bride (the Church) and the Bridegroom (Jesus Christ) will be joined together for all eternity. One of the best descriptions I have heard of the Old Testament is this: *God's wonderful storybook.*

O God, You have given me a most wonderful storybook. I neglect it at my cost. Help me never to lose sight of its importance. Amen.

History – God's story

FOR READING AND MEDITATION
GALATIANS 3:15–25

'So the law was put in charge to lead us to Christ that we might be justified by faith.' (v.24)

Paul condenses into just 11 verses the story of the Old Testament. It is as if he is describing a mountain range whose peaks are Abraham and Moses, with the highest peak – the Everest – being Jesus Christ. His message is simply this: God's promise to Abraham was confirmed by Moses and fulfilled in Jesus Christ. Paul explains the unity of the Bible, while at the same time giving us a sense that through history God has been at work, pursuing a purpose that might have been unseen at the time but was nevertheless part of an eternal plan. 'There is a great need in the Church today for a Biblical Christian philosophy of history,' writes a contemporary. There is, for history is *His story*.

O Father, the more I learn about the story You are telling, the more I want to learn. Take me deeper into this subject, dear Lord. Amen.

Salvation history

FOR READING AND MEDITATION
ACTS 3:11–26

'He must remain in heaven until the time comes for God to restore everything, as he promised long ago ...' (v.21)

To understand God's universal epic we must realise that He has been at work for an everlasting purpose not only in the centuries after Christ but in the centuries before also. The God of the Bible is the God of history – the history of the Old Testament as well as that of the 2,000 years that have passed since Christ was here on the earth. The Almighty, who calls Himself the God of Abraham, Isaac and Jacob (Exod. 3:6), chose Israel out of many nations to be His covenant people, and came to us in the Person of His Son at a recorded moment in history. The history the Bible recounts is 'salvation history', and the salvation it proclaims was achieved by historical events.

Father, I see Your Word records 'salvation history'. You have been working through history to achieve Your purposes. Truly, history is Your story. Amen.

Taking the long look

FOR READING AND MEDITATION
HEBREWS 6:13–20

'... God wanted to make the unchanging nature of his purpose very clear ...' (v.17)

Henry Ford, in his libel suit with the *Chicago Tribune* in 1919, said, 'History is bunk.' But this view fails to see things from God's perspective, from an *eternal* point of view. Fragments of history tell us very little, but when we take 'the long look' we can see, as C.S. Lewis put it, that history is a story written by the finger of God. Rest assured, my friend. Pause and consider the bigger picture: history is not a random succession of events, each effect having its cause, and each cause having its effect, yet the whole betraying no overall pattern. The God revealed in the Bible is working to a plan and is accomplishing all things according to the purpose of His will (see Eph. 1:11).

Father, help me step back and take in Your whole purpose – to take the long look. In Jesus' name. Amen.

Invitation to a wedding

FOR READING AND MEDITATION
REVELATION 19:1–10

'... the wedding of the Lamb has come, and his bride has made herself ready.' (v.7)

What is the overall story of the Bible? It is a *love story*. God's plan to provide a Bride for His Son is laid down in the types and shadows of the Old Testament. It is unfolded more fully for us by the apostle Paul, and brought into final focus in the passage we have read today. The greatest event in the eternity to come will be the wedding supper of the Lamb. T.S. Eliot penned these depressing words: 'This is the way the world ends. Not with a bang but with a whimper.' For Christians, the end of all things will not be a whimper, but a wedding. We will 'rejoice and be glad ... for the wedding of the Lamb has come'. We who have been wooed by Christ and won to Him will one day be wed to Him. Hallelujah!

O Father, it would be enough to be saved from hell and given a place in heaven. But to be joined to You is amazing. Amen.

The big story of God

FOR READING AND MEDITATION
EPHESIANS 5:22–33

'This is a profound mystery – but I am talking about Christ and the church.' (v.32)

All of us are familiar with the fairy story that tells of a princess who kisses a frog and by so doing turns him into a handsome prince. God's big story is about a Bridegroom touching the lives of stubborn, independent sinners such as you and me, and by His grace turning us into people fit to be joined in marriage to Him, to be His companions for all eternity. What is the 'mystery' that engages Paul's attention here? It is the 'mystery' that just as a married couple become one flesh, so the Church will be one with Christ in eternity. Not a buddy but a bride, not a pal but a partner. This is God's big, eternal love story.

O Father, what a prospect – what a story! We who were deep-dyed sinners but are now washed and made clean, are to be joined with You for ever. Amen.

A divine intimation?

FOR READING AND MEDITATION
GENESIS 2:15–25

'Then the LORD God made a woman from the rib he had taken out of the man, and he brought her to the man.' (v.22)

Dr Cynddylan Jones expressed this viewpoint: 'What happened in the first few pages of the Bible is a dress rehearsal for what takes place in the last few pages of the Bible, when the Church, the Bride of Christ, who was *in* Him and came *out* of Him, will be joined *to* Him in a marriage that will last for all eternity.' In Ephesians 1:4 we are told that God saw us *in* Christ before the foundation of the world. In verse 7 we see that we have redemption through His blood – the blood, you remember, that came from His riven side when a soldier pierced Him with a spear (John 19:34). In Ephesians chapter 5 we read that we who were *in* Him and came *out* of Him will be joined yet again *to* Him.

My Father and my God, one thing is sure: my salvation came from You and my destiny is to be joined to You. Hallelujah! Amen.

The central character

FOR READING AND MEDITATION
MATTHEW 1:18–25

'This is how the birth of Jesus Christ came about ...'
(v.18)

The central character in God's big story is Jesus. 'To see the story of Jesus as confined only to the New Testament,' says one commentator, 'is to misunderstand the purpose of the Bible.' Matthew begins his Gospel with our Lord's genealogy because until we see Christ in the context of His ancestors we will not properly understand His story. Jewish genealogies established the right to belong to the community of God's people. And Jesus' very mission necessitated Him belonging to the people who were to bring blessing to the earth; He was the fulfilment of all the Old Testament promises that related to the Messiah. Jesus has to be seen in the light of a bigger story that goes back many centuries.

Lord Jesus Christ, while I rejoice that You are the central character of Scripture, I am more thankful still that You are the central character in my life. Amen.

'My hero'

FOR READING AND MEDITATION
LUKE 19:1-10

'For the Son of Man came to seek and to save what was lost.' (v.10)

The glory goes not to the ones who are saved but to the One who saves. Some time ago, I watched a television programme featuring the remarkable story of a woman who was saved from drowning on an Australian beach by an ordinary passer-by who couldn't even swim! He received a hero's praise. People who don't know Christ often wonder why we make so much of Jesus. If only they could know the joy of abundant living, of sins forgiven, and, 'of hell subdued and heaven begun'. A preacher I once heard, declared, 'Jesus is my hero'. At first I was slightly offended by the expression. But the more I thought about it the more I realised he was right. Jesus is not only God's hero; He is my hero and role model too.

Lord Jesus Christ, how can I ever thank and praise You enough for saving me and for being such a wonderful Saviour? Amen.

The only Saviour

FOR READING AND MEDITATION
ACTS 4:1–12

'Salvation is found in no-one else, for there is no other name under heaven ... by which we must be saved.' (v.12)

Jesus Christ is not one Saviour among others; He is the *only* Saviour. He is not one of Hinduism's 330 million gods or one of the 40 prophets recognised in the Qur'an. He is not even, in the words of John Stott, 'Jesus the Great, as you might say Napoleon the Great or Alexander the Great'. He continues, 'To us He is the only; He is simply Jesus. Nothing could be added to that; He is unique.' In an age when schools teach that all religions have equal value, we should never forget that Christianity is not one faith among many other faiths; it is in a category all by itself. Christianity is not a religion but a relationship. Jesus Christ is not *a* Saviour, He is the *only* Saviour.

Father, save me from being carried along by the pluralism in today's society and from losing sight of the fact that Jesus is the only Saviour. Amen.

The star of the story

FOR READING AND MEDITATION
MATTHEW 3:13–17

'And a voice from heaven said, "This is my Son, whom I love ..."' (v.17)

There are some who like to downplay Jesus' role, and who regard Christianity as just an ethical system. They speak about the fine principles of the Sermon on the Mount, the Golden Rule, and so on. But Jesus also taught, 'I am the resurrection and the life', and 'Before Abraham was born, I am'. Those lines belong to one Person and one Person alone – our Lord Jesus Christ. Those who regard Christianity as nothing more than moral teaching miss the point. 'Christianity,' said one theologian, 'is Christ.' On Him all the Old Testament truths converge and from Him all the New Testament truths emerge. He is the centre of gravity of the Bible, the hub of the evangel, *the star of God's story*.

Father, Jesus is not only the star of Your story but the star of my story also. Just as You rejoiced in Your Son so do I rejoice in Him too. Amen.

Finitude linked to infinity

FOR READING AND MEDITATION
JOHN 5:16–30

*'Jesus said ... "My Father is always at his work ...
and I, too, am working."' (v.17)*

If we fail to grasp God's story, we will get caught up
in our own story and become preoccupied with self
rather than the Saviour. God's bigger story puts my own
story in context. My finitude is linked to infinity. I must
ask myself: Do I see a story that is much bigger than
my own personal story or do I simply see myself as the
beginning and end of the story? We can also lose the
awareness and thrill of being drawn into the action of
God. The Almighty is at work in the world and we can
work with Him, particularly in developing His salvation
story by telling His story to others. Every believer is
included in God's story, is travelling towards Him and
being drawn closer to Him.

*Father, help me learn the lesson that my life is part of a
bigger story, an eternal story. Help me look at this with the
eyes of kindling faith. Amen.*

Driven – or drawn?

FOR READING AND MEDITATION
MARK 12:18–27

'Jesus replied, "Are you not in error because you do not know the Scriptures or the power of God?"' (v.24)

Another thing that will happen without a grasp of God's story is this: we will treat the Bible as an exegetically precise system and miss its real power. The ancient Sadducees were studious readers of the Scriptures, but they overlooked their main purpose; they were good at alighting on specific texts but, as our reading today tells us, they failed to understand what was really being said. Many Christians' lives are flawless in terms of morality yet are flat in terms of passion. They know how to apply particular Bible texts to life's issues but they cannot see beyond the texts of Scripture to the bigger story. They are driven people rather than drawn people.

Father, help me to examine myself to see whether I am driven by an urge to conform to a code or drawn to live for You because I am caught up in the story You are telling. In Jesus' name. Amen.

No sense of story

FOR READING AND MEDITATION
JOSHUA 4:1–24

*'No sooner had they set their feet on the dry ground than
the waters of the Jordan returned to their place ...' (v.18)*

If Christians have no sense of story – of what one
commentator describes as 'knowing that our private
histories are grafted into the stock of salvation history'
– the waters soon rush back in waves of confusion and
distress. How I wish this message was preached from
more pulpits: God is at work, taking everything that goes
on in our lives and weaving it into His salvation story.
If we do not view the details of our sometimes painful
existence as chapters in God's story then we will easily
fall prey to gloom and pessimism. I know of nothing that
enables us to possess the land of our spiritual inheritance
more effectively than the knowledge that our personal
stories are being woven into God's own story.

*Gracious Father, open my eyes that I might see – really see
– that my personal story is congruent with the story of Your
salvation. Amen.*

Everyone has a part

FOR READING AND MEDITATION
RUTH 1:1–14

*'... there was a famine ... a man from Bethlehem ...
together with his wife and two sons, went to live ... in ...
Moab.' (v.1)*

The interesting thing about the book of Ruth is that
there are no outstanding personalities – no kings,
prophets, judges or priests. It is a simple, ordinary
story about three widows and a farmer whose personal
experiences of everyday life are woven into God's
universal epic. The great characters of the Bible, such
as Abraham, Isaac, Jacob, Joseph, Solomon, David and
Daniel, can be intimidating to ordinary people. 'Surely,'
they say, 'there is no way that I can be included in such
a star-studded cast.' The story of Ruth, as we shall see,
gives the lie to such a viewpoint. Every detail of every
believer's life is part of a universal epic – the story of
salvation. And you are an integral part of that.

*O Father, it is wonderful that the details of my life are being
tied in to the story of salvation ... that I am a part of Your
big story. Amen.*

Three funerals and a wedding

FOR READING AND MEDITATION
RUTH 1:15–22

*'Don't call me Naomi ... Call me Mara, because the
Almighty has made my life very bitter.' (v.20)*

I have heard and read many interesting comments on
Ruth, but none so wonderful as this: 'Ruth was an
inconsequential outsider whose life is essential for telling
the complete story of salvation.' A woman who was
not born into the Jewish faith – an outsider – became
integrated into the larger story of God's people. It is
a story about a famine, three funerals and a wedding!
When Naomi finally arrives back in Bethlehem, she can
only respond to their excitement with words of lament:
'I went away full, but the Lord has brought me back
empty' (v.21). That might sound a very negative thing to
say, but her very emptiness is woven into the plot and
becomes, as we shall discover, the occasion for God's
providence.

*Father, I see that negative feelings or even complaints that
are voiced do not preclude us from contributing to Your
story. Amen.*

No editorial deletion

FOR READING AND MEDITATION
JEREMIAH 20:7–18

'O Lord, you deceived me, and I was deceived;
you overpowered me and prevailed.' (v.7)

N aomi's complaint, we noted, was taken seriously;
it was not deleted from the story, toned down or
spiritualised. Her negative feelings were not edited out of
God's story but integrated into it. Complaints are quite
common in Scripture. Jeremiah's – the one in our reading
today – is probably the best known. Edward F. Campbell
says, 'Not only is complaint tolerated by God but it can
even be the proper stance of a person who takes God
seriously.' Later in the book of Ruth we see that Naomi's
emptiness is reversed when, after the birth of Obed,
Ruth's first child, the women of Bethlehem cry, 'Naomi
has a son!' (4:17). Not Ruth, notice, but Naomi.

Father, I am glad that You did not edit Naomi's complaint
out of the narrative but You took it and used it to
demonstrate Your providence. Amen.

Speaking your own lines

FOR READING AND MEDITATION
RUTH 3:1–18

'Spread the corner of your garment over me, since you are
a kinsman-redeemer.' (v.9)

How did Ruth enter the story? *By making clear what
she wanted.* Ruth does exactly what her mother-
in-law suggests, with one exception. She does not wait
for Boaz to tell her what to do; instead, she takes the
initiative and tells *him* what to do. There are times when
it is right to speak our own lines, not just parrot those
that have been given us by others. Be assured of this:
you will not be excluded from God's story when you
speak the lines that come from your own heart rather
than those that are imposed on you by others. Of
course, it is right to allow ourselves to be coached by
parents, schoolteachers and others, but there are times
when we must be ready to ask for what we want – to
speak our own lines.

*Father, I see that just as You accept complaint, so You
acknowledge creativity also. You do not reject those who
make up their own lines. Amen.*

Not a passive player

FOR READING AND MEDITATION
EZEKIEL 16:1–14

'I spread the corner of my garment over you and covered your nakedness.' (v.8)

R uth's actions involved a common custom as we see from today's verse. I make the point once again: for Ruth to be in God's story it did not follow that she had to be a passive player. Even though she is a foreigner, born outside the boundaries of the covenant nation of Israel, she enters the central action of the story when she steps out of the role in which she was placed by others and, in addition to doing what Naomi instructed, takes the initiative and speaks her own lines. And the consequences of Ruth's courageous actions are astounding. She takes her place in history as the great-grandmother of King David and an ancestor of Jesus Christ, the Messiah.

O Father, help me whenever necessary, to step out and speak the words I feel compelled to speak. In Jesus' name. Amen.

Boaz

FOR READING AND MEDITATION
RUTH 4:1–4

'... no-one has the right to do it except you, and I am next in line.' (v.4)

How did Boaz become part of God's salvation story? By accepting responsibility. Boaz had an opportunity to act responsibly and he seized it, not simply because it was expected of him but because he wanted to. He agreed to marry Ruth according to the custom of levirate marriage by which the nearest male relative married a man's widow (see Deut. 25:5–10). He was the kind of man who was not content to live by the letter of the law, but one who sought ways to put his wealth and position to work on behalf of others. This is demonstrated not only by his treatment of Ruth but also by his concern for the welfare of his workers. In Boaz we find a man who lived not by the letter of the law but by the spirit of it.

O Father, help me to look for creative ways in which I can put all my gifts and abilities to work on behalf of others. Amen.

That is how it should be ...

FOR READING AND MEDITATION
RUTH 4:5–8

'So the kinsman-redeemer said to Boaz, "Buy it yourself."
And he removed his sandal.' (v.8)

Edward F. Campbell describes the role of a redeemer in this way: 'to function on behalf of persons and their property within the circle of the larger family ... to take responsibility for the unfortunate and stand as their supporters and advocates ... to care for those who may not have justice done for them'. The name Boaz means 'strength' or 'substance'. Because Boaz took on the responsibility that came his way, lived up to his name, and did more than was required of him by the law, he became a leading character in a story that has made his name immortal. The energy that pulsed through his soul was other-centred. That is how it should be with everyone who is part of God's story.

My Father and my God, help me to live out my part in Your story and make me a truly other-centred person. In Jesus' name. Amen.

'My utmost for His highest'

FOR READING AND MEDITATION
RUTH 4:9–12

'I have also acquired Ruth ... as my wife, in order to maintain the name of the dead with his property ...' (v.10)

Boaz is a man in whose heart burns a desire not merely to keep to the letter of the law, but to give *all* of himself in the service of others. His concern was not to discover what was the *least* he could do, but what was the *most* he could do. His life motto could have been (to use Oswald Chambers' words) *my utmost for His highest*. Some people use their strength and substance simply to maintain themselves, possibly at the expense of others. The question each one of us must answer is this: Where is the energy that drives our personalities being directed – towards ourselves or others? Some Christians regard their wealth as theirs by right and never consider the fact that with rights come responsibilities.

Loving heavenly Father, may what You pour into me also flow out from me. In Jesus' name I ask it. Amen.

Anyone can get in

FOR READING AND MEDITATION
RUTH 4:13–17

*'And they named him Obed. He was the father of Jesse,
the father of David.' (v.17)*

Today's verse takes us by the hand and leads us from a romantic story to an understanding of how ordinary characters became caught up in a larger story. It says in effect, 'See now how God has woven the things that happened to these characters into the story He is telling – the story of salvation. Ruth became the mother of Obed, who was the father of Jesse, who was the father of David ... from whose line the Messiah Himself was born.' The story of Ruth, therefore, though a narrative in its own right, must not be read in isolation. It is a story which leads us into God's epic. And anyone can get into that story – providing they are willing to come in through the door, which is, of course, Jesus Christ.

O Father, how can I ever thank You enough that I have entered through the door and become part of Your salvation story? Amen.

God's great redemptive range

FOR READING AND MEDITATION
RUTH 4:18–22

'... Boaz the father of Obed, Obed the father of Jesse,
and Jesse the father of David.' (vv.21–22)

Matthew's genealogy is highly unusual because it departs from the normal custom of listing the male line only and includes the names of four women: Tamar, Rahab, Ruth and Solomon's mother, Bathsheba. Tamar tricked her father-in-law into fathering her child (Gen. 38:18). Rahab was a prostitute who lived in Jericho (Josh. 2). Ruth, as we have seen, is referred to several times as a Moabitess – a foreigner. Bathsheba was the wife of Uriah the Hittite, and had an adulterous affair with King David (2 Sam. 11:4).

Commentators have pointed out that each of these women was either foreign, immoral or undesirable, and yet was included in the Messianic family tree. How great is God's redemptive range.

Father, Your skill at turning negatives into positives not only fascinates me but encourages me. Thank You, Father. Amen.

'Thick with names'

FOR READING AND MEDITATION
REVELATION 2:12–17

'I will also give him a white stone with a new name written on it, known only to him who receives it.' (v.17)

Scripture, as someone has put it, is 'thick with names'. In the Bible, names have meanings and often describe the character of the person. Jacob (cheat) became Israel (Prince with God). One day every believer is going to have a new name – a name that perfectly describes the person to whom it has been given. What does all this say to us? God's love extends to details and is a love that delights to minister to us not just corporately but individually. If you find it hard to believe that you will be of consequence in heaven because you feel you are of such little consequence down here on earth then think about this: God has reserved for you a new name which will be given to you because of what you have become.

O Father, the more I see how Your love extends to details, the more my love flows out towards You. Amen.

Christ – God's alphabet

FOR READING AND MEDITATION
REVELATION 1:1–8

'"I am the Alpha and the Omega," says the Lord God ...'
(v.8)

L ovely as the story of Ruth is, it is not the whole
story. The whole story is about the Messiah – the
One whom our text for today describes as the 'Alpha
and Omega' – the beginning and the end. One writer
said: 'Christ is the alphabet out of which God frames
every sentence, every paragraph, and every chapter of
His salvation story.' The story recorded in the book of
Ruth leads us ultimately to Jesus Christ. Though Ruth,
Naomi and Boaz were the participants, it is because
of their relationship to Jesus Christ that they take on
their significance. And it is the same with you and me.
Our life stories become *significant* when, through our
relationship with Jesus Christ, they are woven into
His story.

*Father, thank You that through Your Son's sacrifice for me
on the cross I, an outsider, am now an insider. My name is
on the Saviour's family tree. Hallelujah!*

Accepting the inevitable

FOR READING AND MEDITATION
PSALM 73:1–28

'Surely in vain have I kept my heart pure ...' (v.13)

How should we live as participants in God's big story? First, we must accept the inevitabilities of life. A famous psychiatrist, M. Scott-Peck, began his book *The Road Less Travelled* with these words: 'Life is difficult.' Once we face that fact, he points out, 'once we truly know that life is difficult, then life is no longer difficult. Because once it is accepted, the fact that life is difficult no longer matters. Then we can transcend it.' We have been born into a fallen world, and things inevitably happen that are not to our liking. 'Here,' as a friend of mine puts it, 'there is something wrong with everything; there [speaking of heaven] nothing will be wrong with anything.'

My Father and my God, help me to understand that I live in a fallen world, and teach me how to accept the things I cannot change. Amen.

Don't dam the stream

FOR READING AND MEDITATION
JOB 21:1–21

'Who is the Almighty, that we should serve him?' (v.15)

Some people suffer a crushing loss but never come to terms with it in their hearts. They remain bitter and envy the happiness of others, resenting the good life that those whom they regard as undeserving appear to enjoy. In their hearts they are hostile to God. Job, as we see from the passage we have read today, experienced some moments of antagonism towards God. Dr Barnardo, the founder of Barnado's children's homes in Britain, lost his little son from diphtheria when he was nine years of age. Instead of developing a grudge he resolved to help other destitute children. Are you harbouring a grudge? Dare to surrender it now. Grace may flow like a river but a grudge will dam the stream.

O God, forgive me if a grudge is damming the stream of Your grace. Help me surrender all my grudges to You right now. Amen.

The power of lament

FOR READING AND MEDITATION
PSALM 55:1–23

'My heart is in anguish within me; the terrors of death assail me.' (v.4)

To participate in God's story we must be willing to lament not only our personal pain but also our society's rejection of God. The theme of lament is not popular with the majority of Christians, who seem to think that when a negative feeling arises it is best to pretend it isn't there. Do you realise that 70 per cent of the psalms are laments? These laments arose from the disappointments, losses and tragedies the psalmists faced, because they did not avoid these issues or deny the way things were. Look again at David's words in Psalm 55. He faces everything, and prays through everything. Eugene Peterson claims that 'the craggy majesty and towering dignity of David's life are a product of David's laments.'

My Father and my God, help me understand the importance of lament and giving my soul time to feel the pain. In Jesus' name I pray. Amen.

Lament not grumbling

FOR READING AND MEDITATION
PSALM 64:1–10

'Hear me, O God, as I voice my complaint ...' (v.1)

Dan Allender says: 'Lament is as different from grumbling as a search is from aimless wandering.' A grumbler has already reached a conclusion about life. In contrast, a person uttering a lament is expressing a desire to understand what is happening. Notice how often the psalmists, after they have expressed their pain, fall back into the arms of God and say, 'But as for me, I trust in you' (Psa. 55:23). When you lament you are being real with your emotions, being true to how you feel about what has happened to you. But having expressed your feelings, you then fall back on the certainty that God knows exactly what He is doing. There is a place for lament in the lives of all of us and it has great power.

Teach me the power of lament, my Father, so that I might deal with all my soul's needs in a way that contributes to my spiritual health. Amen.

Knowing God better

FOR READING AND MEDITATION
PSALM 77:1–20

'When I was in distress, I sought the Lord ...' (v.2)

Lament can change our attitudes because it compels us to strip our hearts of all pretence and forces us to wrestle with God, which produces a new awareness of God and a new sense of His presence. There is no guarantee that our questions will be answered, but we will know *Him* better. Why one moment does the psalmist rail against God, and then the next affirm His goodness? This is simply the experience of the soul rising through confusion – even anger – to recognise that, after all, God knows what He is doing and that He is good. We admit how we are feeling, struggle with it, and then move on to acknowledge the greatness and goodness of our God. Lament is an important way of participating in God's story.

O Father, I see that if I want to be involved in Your story then dealing honestly with the affairs of my soul is part of that process. Amen.

How evil can become good

FOR READING AND MEDITATION
PSALM 9:1–10

'I will be glad and rejoice in you ...' (v.2)

Although it is important to lament we must also believe in God's power to change things. Unbelief can hinder (though not outmanoeuvre) even the Almighty. So develop confidence in God's skill at turning life's setbacks into springboards. He can take even the most evil situation and make it work for good. The death of someone you loved, the loss of an investment, a spouse's infidelity, hateful slander – these are things fit only for condemnation. How can one gain by them? The answer is: accept what happens without bitterness, enter into it with lament for an appropriate length of time, and have faith in God's transforming power. You will find that He can bring good out of everything bad.

Father, I believe, help my unbelief. In the midst of pain, confusion and disappointment I look to You to transform me into the image of Jesus. Amen.

When sin recoiled

FOR READING AND MEDITATION
COLOSSIANS 2:6–15

'And having disarmed the powers ... he made a public spectacle of them, triumphing over them by the cross.' (v.15)

God can transform everything that happens and make it work for good – even the worst form of evil. The cross is the supreme example. If God could transform what happened there, He can do the same anywhere. At the cross, He took the foulest thing that has ever occurred and made it into the most sublime. The essence of evil became the highest expression of pure love. If God can do that with the cross what might He not do with the evil that comes into our lives? Will He be beaten by abuse, rampant hatred, crime, loss? No. He will dip His pen in these dark colours and write a story that will transform the evil into good. *God* is telling this story, remember – the greatest story writer in all the universe.

O Father, whenever doubts assail me about Your ability to turn evil to good, help me linger at the cross. Glory be to Your name. Amen.

Entering into mystery

FOR READING AND MEDITATION
JOB 42:1–6

'Surely I spoke of things I did not understand, things too wonderful for me to know.' (v.3)

As participants in God's big story we must be prepared to enter into mystery and celebrate it. Some of God's 'mysterious' purposes, of course, can be explained. However, some things that happen to us cannot be understood, no matter how hard we try to make sense of them, for we are, as C.S. Lewis said, riding 'with our backs to the engine'. Mystery challenges us in the area of trust. So we must enter into the mysteries and celebrate them, trusting that our lives are in safe hands. We enter into mystery by giving up our pathetic struggles to explain the unfathomable God and instead rejoice that God knows more than we do. God is good and we must go on believing that even in the deepest of mysteries.

My Father and my God, take my hand and walk with me through every mysterious situation in which I find myself. Amen.

Rejoice in mystery

FOR READING AND MEDITATION
PSALM 45:1–17

'My heart is stirred by a noble theme as I recite my verses for the king ...' (v.1)

One author says, 'God does not look kindly on our editorial deletions, but He delights in our poetry.' I believe he is thinking of the different approaches that a poet and a prose writer might have to the mysterious. There is a difference between poetry and prose. In nature and purpose they are totally distinct. The prose writer might look at things analytically and say, 'I need more illumination before I can comment.' Poetry is the product of passion. The poet is more likely to respond by entering into the mystery and composing a poem about it. This is what the psalmist is doing in the psalm we have read today. He doesn't attempt to manage the mystery of God; he simply rejoices in it.

O Father, grant that I may respond to what You are doing in my life with the poetry of thanksgiving and praise. Amen.

More about poetry

FOR READING AND MEDITATION
ROMANS 11:25–36

'Oh, the depth of the riches of ... God! How unsearchable his judgments, and his paths beyond tracing out!' (v.33)

When faced with the mystery of God's story in our lives we have two choices: either we respond by trying to figure out God's ways and seek to introduce some 'editorial deletions', or we respond by floating on the waves of His purposes and say, 'Lord, I praise You because Your ways are beyond tracing out', as Paul does in the passage we have just read. Poets recognise mystery and rejoice in it without trying to manage it. Don't try to make sense of mystery when you find yourself caught up in it. Respond poetically to it. Rejoice in it. Blessed are those who allow themselves to be awed by what God is doing in their lives and respond to it with poetic rhythm and praise.

Father, help me to respond to life's mysteries as Paul did – not by attempting to figure things out but by bowing in wonder, love and praise. Amen.

Don't sigh – sing!

FOR READING AND MEDITATION
1 SAMUEL 1:21–2:11

'As surely as you live, my lord, I am the woman who stood here beside you praying to the LORD.' (1:26)

Notice *when* Hannah sang her song – not when Samuel was conceived or born, but when she gave him up to the service of the Lord. Dr Larry Crabb says, 'The deepest and richest songs are sung, not in the moments of blessing, but in those moments when we sense we are being caught up in the movement of God, that we have been lifted into a larger story.' Mary, the mother of Jesus, sang her most sublime song when she realised she was being caught up in a divine movement that would bring salvation to the world (Luke 1:46–55). Are you aware at the moment of something going on in your life that is bigger than your personal agenda – that you are being caught up in a bigger story? Then sing your song!

My Father and my God, whenever I feel called to give something up – help me instead of sighing to sing. In Jesus' name. Amen.

A transcendent drama

FOR READING AND MEDITATION
ISAIAH 38:9–22

'Surely it was for my benefit that I suffered such anguish.'
(v.17)

Whenever I have listened to Joni Eareckson Tada I have heard something inspiring, something of God, about her story. She speaks of suffering that has been redeemed. Joni talks about the events that made her a quadriplegic not in terms of tragedy but in terms of a transcendent drama. She admits, of course, that there was a time of complaint in her life – a time when she shook her fist in God's face – but she has worked through that now and has come to recognise that in allowing her accident to take place, God had a purpose for her life that has touched the lives of millions. How would you tell the story of your life if you were asked, I wonder? As a comedy, a tragedy, an irony or a transcendent drama?

Father, how would I tell my story? As a comedy, a tragedy, an irony or a divine drama? Help me bring glory to You. Amen.

How do I get in?

FOR READING AND MEDITATION
JOHN 3:1–15

'I tell you the truth, no-one can see the kingdom of God unless he is born again.' (v.3)

Today I want to invite those of you who are not yet included in God's salvation story to enter into it. And so I pose this question: How do I enter into a relationship with God and become part of His eternal epic? You enter into a personal relationship with God through His Son Jesus by being what the Bible calls 'born again'. Not a second physical birth but instead a spiritual birth. If you have not been born again I invite you now to open your heart to God and His Son Jesus Christ. Say the following prayer and you will receive the new birth as countless multitudes down the ages have done. You will be born again.

Heavenly Father, I want to be part of Your story. I come to You now to be born again. I surrender everything to You – my whole life, my heart … everything. Accept me and make me Your child. In Jesus' name I pray. Amen.

'In my own voice'

FOR READING AND MEDITATION
COLOSSIANS 1:1–14

'We are asking God that you may see things, as it were, from his point of view ...' (v.9, Phillips)

No matter how insignificant you may feel, if you believe in the Lord Jesus Christ and have been born again, the truth is that you are included in God's big story. Your name is written into His universal epic. One day, when the whole story is unfolded in eternity, you will see what part you have played in the eternal scheme of things. A friend of mine, Phil Greenslade, says, 'I don't mind being just a spear carrier as long as I am part of God's big story.' How different life is when we realise that through all that happens to us a divine story, a bigger story, is being written. I leave you with this line by Paul Goodman, *In my own voice I tell Your story*.

Father help me to see all things from Your point of view. Thank You for the priceless privilege of telling Your story in my own voice. Amen.

A deepening desire

FOR READING AND MEDITATION
JOHN 17:1–10

'Now this is eternal life: that they may know you, the only true God, and Jesus Christ, whom you have sent.' (v.3)

There is in the hearts of Christians everywhere a deepening desire to know more of God. How can we come to know God more fully? We can know God only through the means by which He chooses to reveal Himself: the material creation, the Scriptures, and through His Son, the Lord Jesus Christ. The aim of this series of studies is to discover God more fully through the various names He uses in Scripture. A name, when used in the Bible, is not merely a designation; it is a definition. The names of God reveal His characteristics, and reflecting on them should have a bearing on our own lives and character. As we meditate on God's greatness, His grace and His love, every problem we have falls into its proper place.

Gracious Father, already I sense that over the next two months my hunger for You will be both deepened and satisfied. Amen.

Cosmic backing

FOR READING AND MEDITATION
GENESIS 1:1–13

'In the beginning God created the heavens and the earth.'
(v.1)

The first Hebrew name for God found in the Bible occurs in the opening verse of the book of Genesis: 'In the beginning God created the heavens and the earth.' The name for God here is 'Elohim', and points to the One who possesses all the divine powers. If there is no Creator behind the universe then I cannot be sure that my life has any cosmic backing. I do not know if I am working with anything significant or just working alone and meaninglessly with no one to back my work or even to care. Life cannot be meaningful unless it has meaningful resources. If there is no Creator then life is, indeed, meaningless. If, however, there is a Creator then all of life takes on a new and wondrous meaning.

O God, thank You that my life has cosmic backing. The world just doesn't make sense without You. Amen.

'God's in His heaven …'

FOR READING AND MEDITATION
JOB 23:1–17

'If only I knew where to find him; if only I could go to his dwelling!' (v.3)

When God is not placed firmly in the centre of the universe – His rightful place – we lose the meaning of life. Those who ignore the fact that the universe began through the creative act of a loving God are left with a 'sense of cosmic loneliness'. And those who dismiss God altogether are in an even worse situation for they have no hope of ever coming to terms with a vast universe. As I have mentioned before, an atheist has been described as 'someone with no invisible means of support'. Only as God is given the central place in His universe can the sense of cosmic loneliness be overcome for, to borrow a line from the poet Robert Browning, when God's in His heaven then all's right with the world.

O God, I am so glad that I already know You, and now I yearn to know You more fully. Please help me in my quest. For Jesus' sake. Amen.

'I wish God were back'

FOR READING AND MEDITATION
PHILIPPIANS 3:1–14

'I want to know Christ and the power of his resurrection …' (v.10)

An American minister, who sadly surrendered his Christian faith to the 'God is dead' theory, said in an interview, 'Life is hard and contains little sense or meaning … the heavens are like brass … sometimes I wish God were back'. His case can be likened to that of a man who walks over to a table each day, takes a look at the food, and then turns away in disdain. He could live with this disdainful attitude for a while – but only for a while. In the end the biting pangs of hunger and the weakness he experienced would tell him, even though he refused to eat, that his body was made for food and that to refuse to accept that fact would result in certain death.

Heavenly Father, thank You that because I know You life has meaning and purpose. The heavens are open for us to talk. Amen.

'Searching for me'

FOR READING AND MEDITATION
JOB 22:12–30

*'When men are brought low and you say, "Lift them up!"
then he will save the downcast.' (v.29)*

Without the knowledge that the universe came into being by God's hand, life has no meaning or purpose and everything lacks permanence, stability or reality. We are in the position of being what Sorokin calls a 'sensate society'. It is a society that has exhausted itself against the facts of life. Our age is becoming bankrupt morally, spiritually and financially. When we decide to take a new centre – God – then life for us will have new meaning and new purpose. A one-time agnostic, who passed from agnosticism to faith in Christ, said this: 'I came to the conclusion that the universe did not make sense without God. I set out to search for Him and found that He was searching for me.'

O God, help me to give You Your rightful place at the centre of my universe. Then – and only then – will life make sense. Amen.

Involution – not evolution

FOR READING AND MEDITATION
GENESIS 2:1–7

'… the LORD God formed the man from the dust of the ground
and breathed into his nostrils the breath of life …' (v.7)

As the Creator (Elohim) makes man, He introduces Himself by a new name – the LORD God or, in the Hebrew, Jehovah Elohim. The name 'Jehovah' means 'to be actively present' and contains the thought of faithfulness and unchangeableness. Is it not significant that the first time God is seen in His capacity as the Creator of a human being He is seen as a God who is faithful and who keeps His promises? When God introduced Himself by His personal name He did more than expand His titles; He also revealed to the whole world His deep desire to create beings who could and would reciprocate His love. This is not evolution but involution – God involving Himself in His creation in a distinctively personal way.

O Father, You bend to the dust that I might rise to the highest intention of the universe and have a relationship with the Deity. Amen.

Myth – or reality?

'Now the LORD God had planted a garden in the east, in Eden; and there he put the man he had formed.' (v.8)

Is man the product of a distinctive act of divine creation or is he the result of an evolutionary process? As for myself, I believe the Genesis account to be true – that man was created not by an evolutionary process but by a divine act. Some regard the story as myth, but where does myth end and history begin? Jesus accepted the reality of Adam and Eve's creation (Matt. 19:4) and so do I. If evolution (and not a specific creation) provides the explanation of man's origin then there was no Fall. And if no Fall, no need for salvation or redemption. Fundamental issues are at stake here. Let us put our full weight on the Scriptures and submit our intellects to the authority of God's Word.

O God, hold me fast in the turbulence of current thought and give me a certainty of faith that sustains my heart as well as my intellect. Amen.

'Choose life'

FOR READING AND MEDITATION
DEUTERONOMY 30:15–20

'This day ... I have set before you life and death, blessings and curses. Now choose life, so that you and your children may live ...' (v.19)

The issues of life are before us. We must vote for or against a view of life that has worth, purpose and a goal. If we vote that the universe has no meaning and that there is no distinct purpose running through the story of man's creation then we vote that our own lives have no purpose and no meaning. We are told by psychologists (and it is a fact which is corroborated by the whole of life) that when life has no distinct meaning and purpose then it goes to pieces. How should Christians respond to the theories and philosophies presented by the media and places of education? We listen, evaluate and respect the sincerity of those who teach them, but when called upon to vote – we vote for life.

O God my Father, my vote is for life. I choose life with You as its Creator and Designer, and Your Word, the Bible, as its true exposition. Amen.

Why was I created?

FOR READING AND MEDITATION
PSALM 8:1–9

'… what is man that you are mindful of him, the son of man that you care for him?' (v.4)

When I was involved in counselling I was often asked: 'Why was I created?' Well why does a parent create children? Though procreation is the result of a physical act, in the highest reaches of parenthood it is the result of an impulse to love. Is parenthood different in God? Could God, being love, have done anything other than create objects of that love? And, having created us, will He not give Himself to us? If not, then the whole point and purpose of creation is stultified. God is not just Elohim, the mighty and majestic Creator, but He is Jehovah Elohim – the personal tender and loving Lord who condescends to breathe His life into humankind and extend His arms in the offer of a loving relationship.

O Father, how thrilling it is to be reminded of the divine purpose behind my creation. You made me to know You and live in You. Amen.

El-Shaddai

FOR READING AND MEDITATION
GENESIS 17:1–8

*'When Abram was ninety-nine years old, the LORD
appeared to him and said, "I am God Almighty … "' (v.1)*

Another name of God is El-Shaddai. When Abram's
wife, Sarai, had passed the age of natural child-
bearing, God announces Himself under a new name:
'I am,' He says, 'God Almighty' – 'El-Shaddai'. In the
building of the material universe God announces Himself
as Elohim, the One who possesses all the divine powers.
When breathing His own life into the body of a man,
He reveals Himself as the personal God who is faithful –
Jehovah Elohim. Now, when the destiny of His people,
the children of Israel, is at stake, God steps in, touches
the reproductive system in Sarai's body so that she is
able to have a child and, at the same time, announces
Himself as the great El-Shaddai – the strengthener and
nourisher of His people.

*O God, how reassuring it is to realise that You impart
Your own inner resources to Your people. Your supply so
immeasurably exceeds all human demands. Amen.*

'God the Enough'

FOR READING AND MEDITATION
PSALM 145:1–16

'You open your hand and satisfy the desires of every living thing.' (v.16)

The traditional interpretation of the Hebrew name El-Shaddai is: 'God who is sufficient' or 'God the Enough'. There are many things in this world of which people think they do not have enough. The problem is not so much that people do not have enough of these things but rather that the things themselves are not enough. But perhaps at this very moment you are caught in a situation that to all human intents and purposes seems hopeless. You do not know where to turn. Though you may not always realise it, difficulties and problems are the dark backdrop against which God paints, in vibrant and illuminating colours, the beauty of His infinite care and love. To you, God will be El-Shaddai – 'God the Enough'.

O God my Father, I bow in adoration as You speak to my need today. Your resources so infinitely exceed all my requirements. Amen.

'How great is our God'

FOR READING AND MEDITATION
ISAIAH 40:18–31

'The LORD is the everlasting God, the Creator of the ends of the earth. He will not grow tired or weary ...' (v.28)

Isn't it reassuring to know that God's eternal sufficiency so immeasurably surpasses every demand that we may make upon it? In an age when the world has to consider the possibility of running out of many of its natural resources, we have the comfort of being able to fix our gaze upon the God who created and designed the universe – the God who is *Enough*. Dr Luccock, a writer who was greatly concerned about the increasing amount of traffic on the roads, once said, 'If I die on the streets you can put on my tombstone, "Died of looking the wrong way"'. Many of us are dying spiritually because we are looking the wrong way. Our gaze must be focused continually on God – God the great El-Shaddai, God the Enough.

O God my Father, You alone have the answers that really resolve matters and do not let me down. I gaze on the One who is Enough. Amen.

'Him-possible'

FOR READING AND MEDITATION
GENESIS 17:15–22

'God also said to Abraham, "As for Sarai your wife, you are no longer to call her Sarai; her name will be Sarah."'
(v.15)

At this point not only did God change His own name but He changed Abram's and Sarai's, too. Abram's name became *Abraham* and Sarai's name became *Sarah*. What really was the difference? This: God put an aspirate in their names – the sound of 'h' – part of His own name. The Almighty breathed His supernatural breath into them and to signify this He added an aspirate to their names. The letter 'h' cannot be pronounced without using breath. Try it and see. The great El-Shaddai is always ready to breathe into situations and circumstances where a miracle is required. When He does then the word impossible becomes *Him-possible*. What is not possible to us is indeed gloriously possible to Him.

Gracious God and heavenly Father, breathe into me today so that instead of being weak I shall be strong. In Jesus' name I ask it. Amen.

Jehovah Jireh

FOR READING AND MEDITATION
GENESIS 22:1–14

'So Abraham called that place The LORD Will Provide.' (v.14)

We come now to a series of names beginning with the word Jehovah, the first of which is Jehovah Jireh. We must be careful not to miss the significance of this thrilling revelation. God provides many things for the people He has created. He provides the food we eat, the air we breathe and the light by which we see. But what is His greatest provision? It is atonement for our sin. The term Jehovah Jireh carries with it clear intimations of the sacrificial death at Calvary of Jesus, 'the Lamb of God, who takes away the sin of the world' (John 1:29). It is a signpost directing us to the cross. Abraham, at this moment, looked into the very heart of reality. Only through the cross can we see fully into the heart of God.

Father, help me to see clearly Your provision for my salvation through that great act of love at Calvary. In Jesus' name. Amen.

Hand in hand to heaven

FOR READING AND MEDITATION
PSALM 22:22–31

'They will proclaim his righteousness to a people yet unborn – for he has done it.' (v.31)

Jehovah Jireh, in my opinion, reveals the most about God's character because it gives clear intimations of Christ's death for us. Who was it on that first Good Friday who saw clearly into the heart of God? Was it Peter? No. Was it any of the other disciples? No. It was the dying thief (see Luke 23:40–43). Out of the great crowd who had gathered around the cross, he alone saw into the very heart of reality. He knew little about God, but when he saw the self-giving love of Christ being poured out on those timbers of torture he knew everything. The cross threw back the curtains, letting him see the heart of God. And the result? A robber and the Saviour walked hand in hand into paradise.

O God, I bow before Your cross today in sincere acknowledgement that You really are my Lord and my God. Amen.

Why was man made free?

FOR READING AND MEDITATION
ROMANS 5:6–17

'But God demonstrates his own love for us in this:
While we were still sinners, Christ died for us.' (v.8)

I have often wondered why God dared to create man and to create him free. To give man free will meant that God had to somewhat limit Himself. Suppose that will would go wrong – it would break the human heart and God's heart too, for God would have to live alongside that rebellious, straying human will and still love. But God took the risk on one condition. Anything that fell on man would fall on Him. Speaking of Christ, Paul tells us, 'God made him who had no sin to be sin for us' (2 Cor. 5:21). All love has the desire to make the sins and sorrows of the one it loves its very own. And here, in the unfolding of the name Jehovah Jireh, that most incredible and most glorious truth is beginning to be revealed.

Father, the love that would take such risks and carry its purpose through must inevitably face a cross. Such love has won me for ever. Amen.

Not a needle – a nail

FOR READING AND MEDITATION
ISAIAH 53:1–12

'But he was pierced for our transgressions, he was crushed for our iniquities …' (v.5)

Amy Carmichael was a missionary to India who in 1901 began rescuing children, many of them girls forced into prostitution. One girl caused Amy Carmichael great concern and eventually she took the girl aside and said, 'This is what your rebelliousness is doing to me'. Then Amy plunged a needle into her own arm. As the girl saw the blood spurt out she threw her arms around Amy Carmichael's neck and wept, 'I didn't know that you loved me like that,' and from that moment she was completely changed. Deep down on the inside we all know that our sin has hurt God, but we did not see it clearly until we saw it at the cross. And it was not a needle that our sin drove into God's heart. It was a nail.

O Father, as I gaze again at the cross my heart responds, and I cry out, 'I didn't know You loved me like that'. Thank You, Father. Amen.

Jehovah Rophe

FOR READING AND MEDITATION
EXODUS 15:22–26

'… I am the LORD, who heals you.' (v.26)

Another of God's titles is Jehovah Rophe, which means 'The Lord who heals'. Next to sin, nothing has taken a greater toll on human happiness than illness and disease. It may be, as you read these words now, that your body is racked with pain or you are weighed down with some physical complaint. We can be grateful for all that medical science contributes to our physical health, but when medical science fails there is still God. Indeed, I can testify to the direct healing God gave me when medical help proved ineffectual. Here, in the twenty-first century, over 3,000 years since the words of our text were first uttered, God is still Jehovah Rophe.

O Father, how I need this revelation of Your ability to heal. Let Your health and vitality flow through every part of my being now, I pray. Amen.

Two sources of sickness

FOR READING AND MEDITATION
MATTHEW 8:5–17

*'This was to fulfil what was spoken through the prophet
Isaiah: "He took up our infirmities and carried our
diseases."' (v.17)*

The subject of divine healing presents more problems
than any other subject I know. This is why we must
explore a biblically based philosophy of healing that
can help us cope with this issue. Disease, sickness and
physical disharmony come from two main sources:
(1) actual structural disease brought about by, for
example, heredity, accident, contagion, ignorance, abuse,
poverty and unbalanced nutrition, and (2) functional
disease (which may pass into structural disease) brought
about by incorrect mental, moral and spiritual attitudes.
True Christianity takes both types of illness seriously.
Christianity is founded on the truth of the incarnation:
'The Word became *flesh* and made his dwelling among
us' (John 1:14).

*O Father, You are the God of body as well as soul. Make
this body of mine the finest instrument of Your purposes. For
Jesus' sake. Amen.*

Not the will of God

FOR READING AND MEDITATION
JOHN 10:1–10

'… I have come that they may have life, and have it to the full.' (v.10)

G od does not *will* disease but some forms of illness possibly do arise from God's laws having been broken by us, society, our ancestors or factors in our environment. What is important is that if we are sick we should endeavour to discover whether the illness has come about from a purely structural breakdown or from incorrect or functional attitudes. Most sicknesses by far stem from our negative attitudes to life and are rooted in our emotions. So consider this question: Do your attitudes contribute to physical health? If they do not then in all probability they contribute to sickness and disease. Change those attitudes. Give up resentment, bitterness, worry, anxiety, fear and hate. Believe me, your body will record the difference.

O God, help me to purge from my mind all fear, worry, bitterness, resentment and anxiety so that my body may be well. In Jesus' name. Amen.

How to handle sickness

FOR READING AND MEDITATION
2 CORINTHIANS 12:1–10

'Three times I pleaded with the Lord to take it away from me.' (v.8)

If your sickness is purely physical and does not stem from wrong mental attitudes – what then? If the sickness is serious you should consult a doctor. As God wills health, approach the matter positively and also ask Him to heal you. Pray for your own healing and then, if nothing happens, invite others to join you in prayer. Follow the instruction in James 5:14 and ask church leaders to pray for you. If after prayer and medical help the sickness persists then ask God for His peace and understanding. If the illness goes then all is well. If it remains, with His strengthening and help, we can use it to help develop inward qualities such as patience, endurance, empathy and trust. So either way we win.

O God, I am so glad that when I view life through Your eyes I never lose but always win. Thank You, Father. Amen.

Jehovah Nissi

FOR READING AND MEDITATION
EXODUS 17:8–16

'Moses built an altar and called it The LORD is my Banner.' (v.15)

Today we are introduced to another new name for God – Jehovah Nissi. Following the successful outcome of the battle an altar is built by Moses and a new name of God is connected to it – Jehovah Nissi, meaning 'The Lord is my Banner'. A banner in ancient biblical times was not necessarily a flag such as we use nowadays. The word is translated variously as pole, ensign or standard. It was this staff, the banner of God, which brought the victory. What was the significance of the Amalekites' success when it was lowered and Israel's success when it was raised? This happened in order to impress upon Israel's warring soldiers that only under God's raised banner was victory assured.

O God, how thankful I am that beneath the banner of the cross every spiritual foe can be routed. In Jesus' name. Amen.

'There's a war on!'

FOR READING AND MEDITATION
EXODUS 17:1–8

'The Amalekites came and attacked the Israelites at Rephidim' (v.8)

The Amalekites were descendants of Esau (Gen. 36:12). Though they were defeated at Rephidim they were to become persistent enemies of Israel (Num. 14:43,45; Judg. 3:13; 7:12). This ongoing struggle against the hostile Amalekites is an analogy of the spiritual warfare in which we, God's people, are continually and steadfastly engaged. When men and women take their Christian faith seriously, they can expect spiritual opposition. I am deeply convinced that we will understand life better when we view it as the Bible views it. The Bible says that for every believer there is a war on. But keep in mind that in this war the outcome is already decided: we win.

Gracious Father, I see today that in the midst of this spiritual warfare in which I am engaged You are truly my Jehovah Nissi. Amen.

'Peaceful coexistence'

FOR READING AND MEDITATION
EPHESIANS 6:10–18

'For our struggle is ... against the rulers, against the authorities, against the powers of this dark world ...' (v.12)

At the Red Sea the Israelites were delivered from Egypt's armies by God alone. But they soon discovered that there was a warfare in which they had to fight against the Amalekites. Once we come into the Christian life we must recognise that we are thrust right into the middle of a spiritual battle between the Church and Satan and his forces. For too long many Christians have neglected this fact and have been enjoying a peaceful coexistence pact with the archenemy, the devil. We have adopted this attitude towards Satan: 'Don't bother me and I won't bother you.' The war between Satan and ourselves is not a 'cold war' but a hand-to-hand combat, waged in the power of the Spirit. We should never forget that.

Father, we have been so busy fighting each other that we have been diverted from fighting our real enemy – the devil. Forgive us we pray. Amen.

The finger of God

FOR READING AND MEDITATION
LUKE 11:14–23

'But if I drive out demons by the finger of God, then the kingdom of God has come to you.' (v.20)

Satan will do everything in his power to prevent you from seeing your true authority in Christ. He will try to keep you away from every book, sermon and situation in which you might discover that although he is a cunning and powerful foe, yet, because of what Jesus Christ did for us when He died on Calvary, he is a defeated foe. 'The reason the Son of God appeared was to destroy the devil's work' (1 John 3:8). If you could only see the power that is available to you in Jesus Christ and would reach out to possess it, then, instead of you being afraid of the devil, the devil would be afraid of you. Praise God there is more power in God's little finger than in all the might and energy of Satan and his forces put together.

O God, keep ever before me the thrilling truth that there is more power in one of Your fingers than in the whole of Satan's kingdom. Amen.

Jehovah Qadesh

FOR READING AND MEDITATION
LEVITICUS 20:1–8

'Keep my decrees and follow them. I am the LORD,
who makes you holy.' (v.8)

The next of the Jehovah titles is Jehovah Qadesh. The phrase 'I am the LORD, who makes you holy', as used in our text for today, is in Hebrew 'Jehovah Qadesh' and means 'The Lord who sanctifies'. Its appearance in the book of Leviticus is most appropriate. Leviticus could not be written until Exodus was completed, just as in Christian experience sanctification cannot be achieved until we have experienced the power of salvation. The word 'sanctify' is found over and over again in both Old and New Testament Scriptures. The word 'sanctify' means 'to set apart'. A holy God longs for holiness to be found in His people – in you and in me.

O God, I am willing to give myself to You. So here I am,
Lord. Take me, cleanse me and make me holy. In Jesus'
name. Amen.

What is sanctification?

FOR READING AND MEDITATION
LEVITICUS 20:22–26

'You are to be holy to me because I, the LORD, am holy ...'
(v.26)

The word 'sanctification' means to set something apart, and it is used in four ways in the Old Testament. In Genesis 2:3 it signifies *separation*. In Exodus 13:12 it means to dedicate something to God's use – *dedication*. In Exodus 19:10 it means to cleanse – *purification*. In Exodus 28:41 it means to use something – *ministration*. A Welsh preacher once defined sanctification as 'the action which God takes in order to make His people clean enough to be used by Him'. Perhaps one of the reasons why some of us are not being used by God to the extent that we should is that we have not taken steps to rid ourselves of uncleanness. God desires our holiness today just as much as He did in Old Testament times.

O God, I come to You for cleansing – for deliverance from all uncleanness and sin. Make me pure, dear Lord. In Jesus' name. Amen.

'You clean it – I'll use it'

FOR READING AND MEDITATION
JOHN 17:13–23

'Sanctify them by the truth; your word is truth.' (v.17)

A certain group of Christian young people I knew became concerned about the souls of the other young people in their community, and arranged the screening of a series of evangelistic films in their church. The Spirit appeared to be saying to them, 'You clean it – I'll use it.' So they decided to spend a whole Saturday cleaning, painting, and preparing the upstairs gallery for occupation. On the first night of the evangelistic film showings they held their breath as they saw the church fill up; first the ground floor and then the gallery! Many turned to Christ that night and, as they watched a number come down from the gallery and walk forward in an act of commitment, they remembered the Spirit's instruction: 'You clean it – I'll use it!'

O Father, I confess my need of inner cleansing. Please cleanse me so that I can be fully used. In Jesus' name. Amen.

An act or a process?

FOR READING AND MEDITATION
EPHESIANS 5:15–27

'… Christ loved the church and gave himself up for her to make her holy …' (vv.25–26)

Is sanctification instantaneous or is it a process? There are those who say God sanctifies in a single act, and those who say that sanctification is a process that goes on in our lives day by day. In many ways both views are correct. However we view the matter, one thing is sure: God wants us to be clean, pure and holy. Christ is waiting to deliver us from inbred evil, the stubbornness of self-will, and the self-centred attitudes that leave a dark stain upon our spirits. Let us invite Him to cleanse our inner being from every sin and stain. 'God paints in many colours,' says Gilbert Chesterton, 'but He never paints so gorgeously as when He paints in white.'

Lord Jesus Christ, You purify me as I breathe the air of Your new creation. But I want not just to be cleansed but to be kept clean. Amen.

Jehovah Shalom

FOR READING AND MEDITATION
JUDGES 6:11–24

*'So Gideon built an altar to the Lord there and called it
The Lord is Peace.' (v.24)*

Jehovah Shalom means 'The Lord is Peace'. In this
turbulent period of Israel's history, as depicted in
the book of Judges, God reveals Himself as the 'God of
peace'. After the conquest of the land of Canaan the
Israelites should have entered into a period of rest, but
instead they experienced a great deal of restlessness.
And why? Because they failed to appropriate God's
promises of security and relied on their own energy and
understanding. Perhaps right now you, too, are restless,
nervous, apprehensive and full of fear. Take heart. The
God of this majestic creation is also Jehovah Shalom –
the God of peace.

*O God, You find a way to speak directly to my heart. You
are truly Jehovah Shalom. You are my peace. And I am so
thankful. Amen.*

'Peace of mind'

FOR READING AND MEDITATION
PHILIPPIANS 4:1–13

'And the peace of God, which transcends all understanding, will guard your hearts and your minds in Christ Jesus.' (v.7)

You cannot have peace of mind until you have something deeper than peace of mind. Those who attempt to find peace by different techniques of mental adjustment are doomed to disappointment. When you have peace in the depths of your spirit then peace of mind is an outcome of that deeper peace. In other words, you cannot experience the peace *of* God until you have experienced peace *with* God. No one can experience real peace if there is a conflict in the spirit. We must first experience the joy of sins forgiven and then, and only then, can we know the peace that Paul, in today's text, describes as 'the peace ... which transcends all understanding'. And, for that matter, all misunderstanding also.

O Father, help me to experience, day by day, peace that I do not merely possess but a peace that possesses me. In Jesus' name I ask it. Amen.

Lift the latch

FOR READING AND MEDITATION
JOHN 14:25–31

'Peace I leave with you; my peace I give you. I do not give to you as the world gives.' (v.27)

We are studying the difference between perfect peace, the peace that comes from God, and imperfect peace, the peace that comes from mental tricks. Any peace resulting from mental exercises will inevitably let you down. The peace that comes from God, however, holds up because it has the God of the universe behind it – God's peace. God's peace can stand anything that challenges it. Since it is possible in this restless age to experience the peace of God do not let anything prevent you allowing peace to invade you. Peace is knocking at the door. Lift the latch and let it come in. Make it your life affirmation to say: the peace of God helps me; the peace of God holds me; the peace of God protects me.

O God, help me to live in You, to abide in You, for I know that when I am in You and You are in me then I can meet anything that comes. Amen.

'His rest'

FOR READING AND MEDITATION
COLOSSIANS 3:12–25

*'Let the peace of Christ rule in your hearts, since as
members of one body you were called to peace.' (v.15)*

The book of Hebrews speaks of 'his rest' (4:1). After
the conquest of Canaan the Israelites should have
entered into 'his rest' – a rest foreshadowing that
referred to in Hebrews 4:1. But because of disobedience
they failed to gain that rest. How sad it is that millions of
Christians, who have been freed from bondage also fail to
enter into the rest provided for them by Jehovah Shalom.
In Hebrews 4:9 this rest is spoken of as a Sabbath rest
because the Sabbath was a day when work and struggle
ceased; for us it is a day to accept the gifts of God, to
be quiet and receptive. Don't struggle to gain peace by
attainment; all you need to do is to empty your hands
and take the gift.

*O Father, breathe upon me Your best gift – the gift of the
Holy Spirit who provides me with adequate power and
perfect peace. Amen.*

Jehovah Rohe

FOR READING AND MEDITATION
PSALM 23:1–6

'The LORD is my shepherd, I shall not be in want.' (v.1)

Verse 1 introduces Jehovah Rohe – the Lord my Shepherd. But the words 'I shall not be in want' lead us to think of Him as Jehovah Jireh, the Lord who will provide. Verse 2 is a perfect picture of Jehovah Shalom – the Lord who is peace. The words, 'He restores my soul' (v.3) cause us to think of Jehovah Rophe, the Lord who heals. As He leads us He becomes our Jehovah Tsidkenu, the Lord our Righteousness (v.3). In 'the valley of the shadow of death' (v.4) He becomes Jehovah Shammah, the Lord who is always there. The preparation of the table (v.5) indicates He is Jehovah Nissi, the Lord our Banner. And the anointing of our heads with oil (v.5) reminds us that He is Jehovah Qadesh, the Lord who sanctifies.

O Father, how can I sufficiently thank You for the revelation of Your love contained in this matchless psalm? Amen.

The Good Shepherd

FOR READING AND MEDITATION
PSALM 23:1–6

'Surely goodness and love will follow me all the days of my life ...' (v.6)

In the revelation of Himself as Jehovah Rohe, God is seeking to show us that everything a good shepherd is to his sheep God is to His people, and indeed He is *my* shepherd, the shepherd of *each one* of His people. It is difficult for those of us who live in the West to understand the loving and tender relationship that an Eastern shepherd has with his sheep. Such a shepherd lives with his sheep night and day, cares for them as if they were his children, and calls each one of them by name. Again I say that everything a good shepherd is to his sheep Jehovah is to His people. If such a tender intimacy can exist between a shepherd and his sheep, how much more so between Jehovah and His redeemed children.

O God, You are the Good Shepherd, but more, You are my shepherd and Your guiding hand is over my life. In Jesus' name. Amen.

Ways in which God guides

FOR READING AND MEDITATION
PSALM 31:1–15

'Since you are my rock and my fortress, for the sake of your name lead and guide me.' (v.3)

On their earthly pilgrimage God guides His sheep by suiting His guidance to their individual need. Sometimes He guides us through circumstances but also through those with whom He brings us in contact. This may be through individuals but perhaps more often through the group of believers with whom we have Christian fellowship. More and more I believe that God is speaking to this generation through groups. The play of mind upon mind, attitude upon attitude, method upon method, generates a body of ideas and conclusions that point the way into the future. The correction and support given by a fellowship helps to keep the individual from going astray.

O God, I thank You for those You have brought into my life who have helped me with a kindly word and their deep insight. Amen.

More about guidance

FOR READING AND MEDITATION
PSALM 25:1–14

'He guides the humble in what is right and teaches them his way.' (v.9)

We are looking at ways in which our Good Shepherd guides His sheep. God guides also through our own spiritually developed reason and discernment. Any scheme of guidance that neglects the mind is not helpful. God wants us to love Him with the whole of our being – including the mind. Another way God guides us is through the inner witness of His Spirit to our hearts. Some call it the 'Inner Voice'. For instance, Peter heard it when instructed to go to the Gentiles (Acts 10:19–20). Finally, however, we must always remember that God's chief way of directing us is through the Scriptures. If you ever receive any 'guidance' that is contrary to the Scriptures then think again because God never guides in opposition to His Word.

O God, You who guide me in so many loving ways, help me to check everything against the Scriptures. Amen.

Adonai

FOR READING AND MEDITATION
ISAIAH 6:1–13

*'In the year that King Uzziah died, I saw the Lord seated
on a throne, high and exalted …' (v.1)*

Another name for God is Adonai. The literal meaning
of Adonai is 'Lord and Master', and the word
contains the thought of ownership, lordship and divine
authority. Following the death of King Uzziah in 740 BC
after a long and prosperous reign, a period of national
darkness settled upon Judah. In the midst of the crisis,
however, Isaiah is given a vision of an eternal throne on
which sits the Lord and Master of the universe. It is as
if the Almighty is saying, 'The throne of Judah may be
empty and its occupant dead but such is the nature of
Adonai's throne that it is never unoccupied and never
unattended.' Sometimes we do not see God as Adonai
until an earthly power has failed.

*O God my Father, I see more clearly every day that my
only true security is found in You. Help me to say with the
psalmist, 'I seek you with all my heart …' (Psa. 119:10).
Amen.*

'The everlasting arms'

FOR READING AND MEDITATION
DEUTERONOMY 33:20–29

'The eternal God is your refuge, and underneath are the everlasting arms.' (v.27)

Isaiah said: 'In the year that King Uzziah died, I saw the Lord' (Isa. 6:1). Some commentators believe that Isaiah had allowed his hopes and expectations to become so entwined around the godly King Uzziah that when he was removed those hopes toppled and his expectations died. I wonder, am I talking to someone today who over the past few weeks and months has been experiencing a removal of the props that support their life? God is not indifferent to your needs. Sometimes, though, it's when the props fall away from under our feet that we then rest our weight fully upon Him. We may need to be willing to see our earthly securities buried before we can see the glory of the heavenly King who sits upon the throne.

O God, I see so clearly that You allow the support to give way beneath my feet in order that I might know the greater security of Your everlasting arms. Amen.

'Let us be grateful'

FOR READING AND MEDITATION
ISAIAH 12:1–6

'Surely God is my salvation; I will trust and not be afraid.' (v.2)

Some time ago when there were reports of an oil crisis, I turned to my Bible and came across some words that have become exceedingly precious to me over the past few years: 'Let us be grateful for receiving a kingdom that cannot be shaken … ' (Heb. 12:28, RSV). All around us at the moment there is a great shaking of earthly values and earthly kingdoms. This is the time, I believe, that God wants us to look up and see that He is still Adonai – the Lord of the universe and Master of every situation. He is allowing kingdoms to be shaken so that men and women might discover the one kingdom that is unshakeable – the kingdom of our God and of His Son, the Lord Jesus Christ.

O Father, what comfort it gives me to realise that I belong to an unchanging Person and an unshakeable kingdom. I am eternally grateful. Amen.

'In this year'

FOR READING AND MEDITATION
ISAIAH 43:8–21

'See, I am doing a new thing! Now it springs up; do you not perceive it?' (v.19)

Taking a more personal perspective for a moment, I wonder, as you look back over the past twelve months, what kind of a year it has been for you. Has there been an upheaval resulting in the loss of many of the things on which your security was based? Have you experienced, as Isaiah did, an end to your hopes, your expectations and your ambitions? Then take heart, for a new vision of God is about to break upon you. You will be able to say, as did the great prophet, 'In the year that my hopes vanished, my security was destroyed and my expectations came to nothing, in that year ... "*I saw the Lord*"' (Isa. 6:1).

O God, help me, before this year ends, to see a new vision of You – a vision that will send me singing into the future. In Christ's name. Amen.

Jehovah Tsidkenu

FOR READING AND MEDITATION
JEREMIAH 23:1–8

'This is the name by which he will be called: The LORD Our Righteousness.' (v.6)

The title Jehovah Tsidkenu is revealed for the first time in one of Jeremiah's stirring prophecies – amid this dark, sombre setting of Judah's sin and failure, a new name for God shines out: Jehovah Tsidkenu – the Lord our Righteousness. The word *tsidkenu* is derived from the Hebrew word *tsedek*, which means 'to be straight'. Pious Jews such as the Pharisees wanted more than anything to be righteous, but their righteousness often turned into a legal righteousness intent on obeying laws instead of a life righteousness eagerly obeying principles. The promise is given, however, that One will come who will make men and women righteous according to His righteousness – a righteousness that blends with life.

O God, save me from the righteousness of the Pharisees that is nothing more than legal enslavement. Give me, I pray, Your righteousness. Amen.

God's handwriting

FOR READING AND MEDITATION
EXODUS 20:1–17; 31:18

'When the LORD finished speaking to Moses on Mount Sinai, he gave him … the tablets of stone inscribed by the finger of God.' (31:18)

The first time God wrote to men and women was when He wrote the Ten Commandments on the top of Mount Sinai. Then, as our text for today tells us, God inscribed with His own finger the words of the Ten Commandments on tablets of solid stone. What He wrote reveals His character in the clearest of ways. His writing at Sinai says this: God is holy. Other nations knew that God was powerful. They saw Him in the thunder and in the lightning and concluded that He was the personification of powerful unseen forces. But it was the Hebrews who grasped the sublime truth that the greatest thing about God is not His might but His moral character.

O God, since the greatest thing about You is Your moral character, may I possess this same quality, too. In Jesus' name I ask it. Amen.

Belshazzar's feast

FOR READING AND MEDITATION
DANIEL 5:1–9

'Suddenly the fingers of a human hand appeared and wrote on the plaster of the wall …' (v.5)

God's handwriting cannot be understood but Daniel, one of God's servants, interprets it as meaning, 'You have been weighed on the scales and found wanting' (v.27). Once again the truth comes over clearly in the handwriting on Belshazzar's palace wall – God is righteous. Now if God is righteous it follows that those who approach Him and seek to gain His favour must themselves become righteous. Yet how can human beings, tainted as they are by sin, obtain a righteousness that will satisfy the demands of a holy God? It is precisely at this point that Jeremiah's promise, which we discussed two days ago, brings a ray of hope. The righteousness He demands of us He, Himself, provides. Hallelujah!

O God, because of the righteousness that comes to me through Jesus, Your Son, I am no longer separated from You by my sin. Hallelujah!

God obeys His own laws

FOR READING AND MEDITATION
JEREMIAH 33:15–26

'In those days Judah will be saved … This is the name by which it will be called: The LORD Our Righteousness.' (v.16)

We have been seeing that God's righteousness is an essential part of His character. This means that morality is rooted not in the will of God but in the nature of God. In giving the promise of One who would come whose righteousness would cover the nakedness of the human condition, God does everything that He commands us to do. He obeys His own laws of right and wrong. He commands us to obey them because He Himself does so – obeys them because they are inherently right. The Almighty is not a cosmic signpost pointing the way; He is a shepherd who goes before His sheep and leads them. A Messiah would come and wear my flesh, measure its frailty and provide me with a righteousness that would satisfy the highest demands of a holy God.

O Father, what delight it gives me as I look into the face of Jesus to see there a consistent God. Since morality is rooted in You it shall be rooted in me. Amen.

Jehovah Shammah

FOR READING AND MEDITATION
EZEKIEL 48:30–35

'And the name of the city from that time on will be:
THE LORD IS THERE.*' (v.35)*

The last of the Jehovah titles – Jehovah Shammah – means 'The Lord is there'. When the people of Israel, in captivity in Babylon, are at their lowest ebb, God breaks into the situation and reassures them. The nation would experience a revival and a restoration in a measure far beyond anything it had experienced in the past or could have ever imagined. It is as if God is telling His people that whatever lay ahead of them, whatever circumstance or situation they would meet, they should never forget that the God who brought them out of Egypt is also Jehovah Shammah – always there. He would be with His people for ever. Are you about to face a difficult day? Then take heart. Remember, the Lord will be there.

O God, how I praise You for the unutterable peace that possesses me when I realise that, no matter what lies ahead, You will always be there. Amen.

'Nor the future ...'

FOR READING AND MEDITATION
ROMANS 8:31–39

'... neither the present nor the future ... will be able to separate us from the love of God that is in Christ Jesus our Lord.' (vv.38–39)

An Athenian orator writing in the second century to the Emperor Hadrian said, 'These Christians who know and trust their God are prepared for anything that comes their way for they believe that no matter what happens to them in the future, their God will always be there.' Notice the words *their God will always be there.* What a thought with which to face the future! Followers of Jesus Christ in every age have clung to a simple truth that, though oft repeated, still carries a powerful message: we may not know what the future holds but we know who holds the future. Although society may undergo enormous change, Jesus remains 'the same yesterday and today and for ever' (Heb. 13:8).

Father, I see that You are wanting to free me from the paralysis of wondering what tomorrow holds and instead give me the power to live one day at a time. Amen.

'One grain of sand'

FOR READING AND MEDITATION
MATTHEW 6:24–34

'Therefore do not worry about tomorrow, for tomorrow will worry about itself.' (v.34)

In my teens I was extremely apprehensive of the days that lay ahead. But then a man took me aside and gave me this advice: 'Think of your life as an hour glass. There are thousands of grains of sand in the top of the glass and they all pass slowly and evenly through the narrow neck without impairing the glass in any way. Take life a grain at a time and let the grains pass through the day slowly and evenly. If you do not take them one at a time then you will impair your own physical and mental structure.' That guidance had a profound effect upon me and completely changed my life. And I have practised that simple philosophy ever since: 'One grain of sand at a time.' Surrender tomorrow into the hands of Jehovah Shammah, the God who is there.

Gracious God, my Jehovah Shammah, I commit into Your hands all my tomorrows so I will not be numbed by fear or apprehension. Amen.

What He was He is

FOR READING AND MEDITATION
ISAIAH 43:1–7

'When you pass through the waters, I will be with you …
For I am the LORD, your God …' (vv.2–3)

A Christian who fails to see that God is Jehovah Shammah, the God who is there, will tend to live on a diet of finger nails rather than a diet of faith. Biting your nails because you are worried about tomorrow is not nourishing; it gets you into the raw. God is always there ready to fulfil His eternal promises. The God who promised that the nation of Israel would be restored and revived – has He not kept His word? If you are afraid of the future and wonder whether or not God will be there in the days, weeks, months and years that lie ahead then take courage from the fact that what He is, He was, and what He was, He is, and what He was and is, He ever will be – world without end.

Father, burn upon my heart the fact that because You are Jehovah Shammah the future can hold no fear for me if we travel together. Amen.

The name of Jesus

FOR READING AND MEDITATION
MATTHEW 1:18–25

'... you are to give him the name Jesus, because he will save his people from their sins.' (v.21)

E ven the divine titles fail to fully reveal God. A life had to come among us – a divine life – in order to put a new content into the words used to describe God, and illustrate them in ways that we cannot fail to understand. This is what happened in the incarnation. God came into the world in the Person of His Son, who took on a human life and proceeded to live out that life in a way that fully revealed His Father's heart. The literal meaning of the name Jesus is 'Jehovah saves'. It gathers up in itself the attributes of God's character and presents them in a name that is at once warm, endearing and human. When we look at God through Jesus we see Him not only as a great Creator, but more – a great Saviour.

Lord Jesus, thank You for putting a face on God and for showing me that the greatest characteristic of the Deity is not the power to create but the power to save. Amen.

God as He really is

FOR READING AND MEDITATION
JOHN 1:1–5

'In the beginning was the Word, and the Word was with God, and the Word was God.' (v.1)

Down the ages God has revealed Himself in different ways. He has revealed Himself through nature (Acts 14:17; Rom. 1:19–20). But not perfectly. He has revealed Himself through prophets and teachers (2 Kings 17:13; Psa. 103:7). But not perfectly. In both cases the medium of revelation was imperfect. When He revealed Himself through His Son – 'the Word become flesh' – then for the first time God found a perfect vehicle of communication. In Jesus we see God as He really is. Why does John refer to Jesus Christ as the *Word*? Well, words are the expression of a hidden thought. Jesus is the expression of the invisible God. Without the incarnation we would still be left wondering what God is really like.

O Father, I realise today that as I take hold of Your Word, I take hold of Your highest thought. And that highest thought is love. Amen.

He made His dwelling among us

FOR READING AND MEDITATION
TITUS 2:1–15

'For the grace of God that brings salvation has appeared to all men.' (v.11)

Consider the words 'and made his dwelling among us'. This revelation of God was not like the momentary disclosures of the Old Testament. The only way God could redeem His people was to come to them. Did He choose to save us by sitting on a cloud and uttering commands or by picking us up and transferring us to heaven in the grip of celestial tongs, thus not soiling His fingers with the messy business of human living? No. Jesus made His dwelling among us – amid our poverty, our misery, our temptations, our problems, our choices, our opposition and our disappointments. He lived among us, wore our flesh, felt our pains, and showed us by a sustained, day-by-day revelation what God is really like.

Lord, You came to where I was in order to take me to where You are. You came to show life in the midst of life. Thank You, Lord Jesus. Amen.

He has been made known

FOR READING AND MEDITATION
JOHN 1:1–18

'... *God the One and Only, who is at the Father's side, has made him known.*' (v.18)

You cannot describe God, or even define Him, but He can be shown. And Jesus did just that. He made Him known in the only way He can be known – by revealing His innermost character. What is the central thing about God? Is it not His character? The words 'in the bosom of the Father' found in the New King James Version suggest that Jesus has made God's heart known to us. Jesus is not depicted here in the arms of the Father – that would reveal only His omnipotence. He is not spoken of as in the mind of the Father – that would reveal His omniscience. He is 'in the bosom of the Father' and, because of this, He is able to reveal the innermost heart of the Deity. And that heart is a heart of love.

O God, I am thankful that I find in You the love I so desperately need. I would never have found it unless I had been shown it – shown it in Your Son. Amen.

Father and Mother

FOR READING AND MEDITATION
JOHN 1:6–14

'We have seen his glory, the glory of the One and Only, who came from the Father, full of grace and truth.' (v.14)

The nature of fatherly love is that it makes demands, establishes clear rules or laws, and takes a firm grip on the one it loves as well as protecting and providing. Motherly love is somewhat different; at its highest level it is unconditional, nurturing, all-protective and all-enveloping. Our text tells us that in Christ both of these are to be found. He is 'grace' and He is 'truth'. Grace is the motherly characteristic and truth is the fatherly characteristic. For example, He died for sinners but condemned the Pharisees. A careful examination of the nature of our Lord leads us to the firm conclusion that in the incarnate Son we see both the Fatherhood and the Motherhood of God.

Father, as I look at You through Jesus, Your Son, I see You as strict yet saving, terrible yet tender, and I am grateful for both. Amen.

Christmas begins with Christ

FOR READING AND MEDITATION
LUKE 2:1–17

'Today in the town of David a Saviour has been born to you; he is Christ the Lord.' (v.11)

We come to Christmas Day – a day when we joyfully celebrate the coming of our Lord Jesus Christ to this earth. The message of Christmas is this: there is only one way that God can be found and that is through Jesus, the Babe of Bethlehem. Some try to find God through nature – the nature worshippers. Some attempt to find Him within themselves – the 'ego' worshippers. Still others attempt to find Him through teachers and gurus – the men worshippers. But if you want to find God – to really find Him – then you must come face to face with His Son, Jesus Christ. Jesus is God approachable, God available, God lovable. Begin Christmas by looking not at the sparkle but at the Saviour. Look into the face of Jesus and live.

Gracious God, just as I cannot say the word 'Christmas' without first saying 'Christ' I cannot really find You until I first come face to face with Him. Amen.

Jesus – the only way

FOR READING AND MEDITATION
JOHN 14:1–14

'Jesus answered, "I am the way and the truth and the life. No-one comes to the Father except through me."' (v.6)

There have been two great attempts to find God apart from Christ – they are the ways of philosophy and moralising. Both failed in their quest. Into a world troubled by these doubts and difficulties, Jesus came and announced, 'I am the way and the truth and the life. No-one comes to the Father except through me.' The philosophers and the moralists could not find the way for there is no way created by mere words. The only way is 'the Word become flesh'. 'Jesus', said a well-known Bible commentator, 'is God's other name.' A missionary being helped through the thick and almost impenetrable African bush by a local guide asked, 'Is this the way?' 'No,' replied the guide, 'I am the way.'

O Father, how simple is the message of the gospel. I follow You as the way, the way directs me to the truth, and the truth leads to life – life eternal. Amen.

'I am the gate'

FOR READING AND MEDITATION
JOHN 10:1–14

'I am the gate; whoever enters through me will be saved.'
(v.9)

It might not have been possible for the Old Testament saints to fully understand the meaning of the august title God revealed to Moses, 'I am who I am'. This great name of God never seemed to have a clear definition, but now all that is changed. Jesus takes that vague name of God and gives it clear identity by stating that He is a 'gate', a 'shepherd', a 'light', and so forth. 'I am the good shepherd,' He says (v.11). 'I am the light of the world' (8:12). 'I am the way and the truth and the life' (14:6). Through Jesus the great name of God, 'I am', opens out into the most wonderful, the most exciting of all revelations – that He is the only way by which men and women can know and understand God.

Lord Jesus Christ, You have clarified our understanding of God by taking His great name and linking it to objects that I can clearly comprehend. Amen.

A word become word

FOR READING AND MEDITATION
I TIMOTHY 3:16–4:9

'He appeared in a body, was vindicated by the Spirit …
was believed on in the world, was taken up in glory.' (3:16)

When confronted by the religions of the East, everything the missionary Dr E. Stanley Jones talked about had its parallel. Then it dawned upon him that all that had been said by the Muslim and the Hindu was simply a word become word. Their stories were illustrations, not exhibitions. The other stories, too, were illustrations, not reality. The difference between the Christian faith and other religions is that other religions are a word become word, whereas the Christian faith is a Word become flesh. Jesus was actually God who became a man and was crucified. This makes the Christian faith not just a little better than other faiths; it sets it on a level where no comparisons are possible.

Lord Jesus Christ, the fact that You became flesh astounds me. You have gone further than I dreamed possible. Thank You, dear Lord. Amen.

Not just better – different

FOR READING AND MEDITATION
PHILIPPIANS 2:1–11

'Who, being in very nature God ... made himself nothing, taking the very nature of a servant, being made in human likeness.' (vv.6–7)

The Christian faith is unique because it has at its heart the incarnation. The Christian faith is not just better than every other faith – a little more moral, a little more lofty in its concepts – it is completely different. All other religions tell of man's search for God; Christianity tells of God's search for man – of the One who 'came to seek and to save what was lost' (Luke 19:10). This is why, though there are many religions, there is only one gospel. The world's religions tell of the word become word; the gospel is the Word become flesh. In the face of all rivals our gospel quietly affirms, 'The Word became flesh and made his dwelling among us. We have seen his glory ...' (John 1:14).

Father, I realise that my salvation came not because of my knocking on the door of heaven but because You knocked at the door of my heart. Amen.

Christ – the perfect revelation

FOR READING AND MEDITATION
MATTHEW 13:1–17

'But blessed are your eyes because they see, and your ears because they hear.' (v.16)

Suppose God had decided against an incarnation and instead had given us a book similar to the Bible as His highest revelation – what would be the result? We would attempt to read into those words our highest interpretation but nevertheless we would be greatly limited. Take the word 'God'. Were it not for the incarnation I would interpret the word in the light of my imagination, but now, because Christ has come, I look up through Jesus, the Son of God, and I know without any shadow of doubt what God is like. The apostle Paul reminds us that Jesus 'is the image of the invisible God, the firstborn over all creation' (Col. 1:15). 'Anyone who has seen me has seen the Father,' Jesus assures us (John 14:9).

Blessed Jesus, I am so thankful to You for showing me the Father. I would never have known what He is like had I not looked into Your face. Amen.

His name – our name

FOR READING AND MEDITATION
REVELATION 22:1–7

'They will see his face, and his name will be on their foreheads.' (v.4)

The Holy Spirit directs our attention in the last chapter of the Bible to a breathtaking and vibrant truth: *one day God's name is to become our name!* What a tremendous note on which to end our studies: 'They will see his face, and his name will be on their foreheads.' At this moment all the privileges of His name are ours – salvation, healing, cleansing, sanctification. But in eternity all these characteristics, instead of being available to us, will become an integral part of us because when we see God we shall be like Him (1 John 3:2). Then His virtue will become ours, His victory will become ours, His nature will become ours and, what is more, His name will become ours. For ever and ever. Amen.

O Father, to be given Your name in eternity and to carry it in my own personality is a truth that staggers my imagination. All I can say is thank You, Father. Amen.

More encouragement in this series

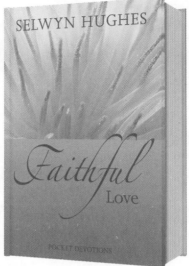

Topics covered:
- *Unveiled Faces*
- *Our Lord at Prayer*
- *A Fresh Look at the Church*
- *The Blessed Life*
- *Life Convictions*
- *Surprised by God*

Makes a welcome gift!

374-page hardback, 152x100mm
ISBN: 978-1-85345-602-2

For current price visit www.cwr.org.uk/store
Also available from your local Christian bookshop.

Courses and seminars

Publishing and new media

Conference facilities

Transforming lives

CWR's vision is to enable people to experience personal transformation through applying God's Word to their lives and relationships.

Our Bible-based training and resources help people around the world to:
• Grow in their walk with God
• Understand and apply Scripture to their lives
• Resource themselves and their church
• Develop pastoral care and counselling skills
• Train for leadership
• Strengthen relationships, marriage and family life and much more.

 Applying God's Word *to everyday life and relationships*

CWR, Waverley Abbey House,
Waverley Lane, Farnham,
Surrey GU9 8EP, UK

Telephone: +44 (0)1252 784700
Email: info@cwr.org.uk
Website: www.cwr.org.uk

Registered Charity No 294387
Company Registration No 1990308

Our insightful writers provide daily Bible-reading notes and other resources for all ages, and our experienced course designers and presenters have gained an international reputation for excellence and effectiveness.

CWR's Training and Conference Centre in Surrey, England, provides excellent facilities in an idyllic setting – ideal for both learning and spiritual refreshment.